THE SATANIC REBELLION

And the Heavenly Realms

S C SAYLES

To Vic
DRINK DEEP
OR TOUCH NOT
THE SACRED SPRING

Seek q/

1

THE SATANIC REBELLION

And the Heavenly Realms

S C SAYLES

THE SATANIC REBELLION

And the Heavenly Realms

S C SAYLES

PUBLISHED BY EVOLSIAY TULIP

Author: S C SAYLES
Coverdesign: S C SAYLES
ISBN: 9781720183181

Other books by S C SAYLES

**HIGHER DIMENSIONS & METAPHYSICAL ANTHROPOLOGY:
A BIBLICAL PHILOSOPHY**

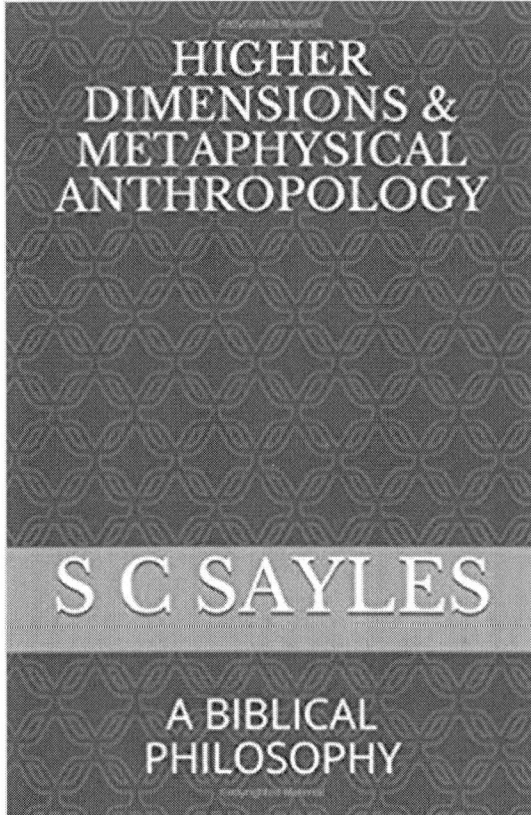

S C Sayles explains the true nature of the "theoretical" higher dimension hypothesis. Exploring the true nature of homo sapiens, death, life and "otherworldly" entities. This is a fascinating and insightful book.

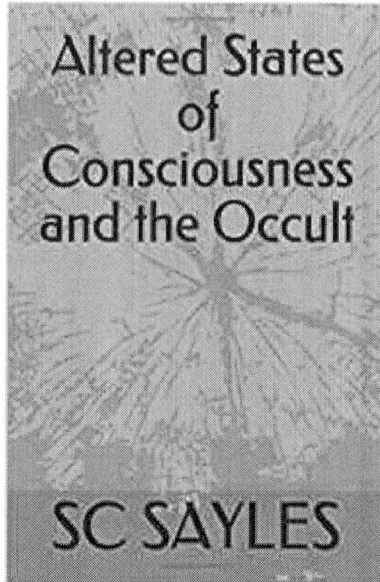

The phenomenon that we have come to know as the paranormal is far from modern. Many identical stories and similar strange events and practices can be found in all cultures and ages. There are many types of occult practices such as, hypnotism, transcendental meditation, astral projection, channeling, necromancy, alien abduction.poltergeist activity, visionary experiences, demon possession,Shamanism, Transcendental Meditation (TM), Unitive Consciousness, Ego-Transcendence, Cosmic Consciousness, Zen , Nam Sumran, Tantristic, Spiritualism, Astral Projection, Remote Viewing etc. In this well researched book SC Sayles presents a definite connection between Altered States of Consciousness and the Occult. This book is informative and serves as a warning to the dangers invoked when entering into Altered States of Consciousness.

SC SAYLES

THE WALLS COME TUMBLING DOWN

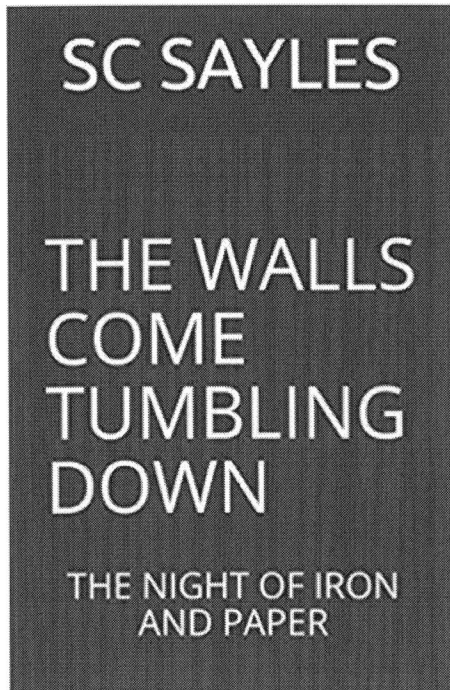

THE NIGHT OF IRON AND PAPER

From Descartes to Kant. Plato to Freud. Drug abuse and occultism. Eastern Philosophy to science, Steve was on a mission of discovery, a journey to uncover the nature of reality. Was he truly seeking to understand the phenomena' of everyday reality or was he actually in a battle for sanity? One event held the key. The Night of Iron Paper held the key but it was also the doorway to madness and terrifying insanity.

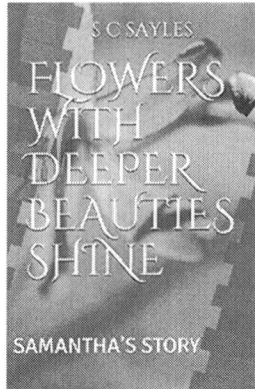

Samantha struggled with her past. The abuse haunted her in the present. She saw suicide as her future. Samantha's life was a nightmare. She would often see her friends walking with their daddies and felt a pang of jealousy. 'Why can't my life be like that' she cried in her thoughts. Her dad would take every opportunity to touch her. Samantha felt disgusting and hated herself. While the abuse was happening she would focus all her attention on a particular spot on the wall or ceiling, making herself 'go away'. Oh she wished she could really go away. To leave the parents who hated her. One afternoon Samantha was in the house on her own. While looking out of the bedroom window she noticed a blackbird flying to and fro the nest. 'Dad loves those birds' she mused. 'He would be gutted if anything should happen to them' her thoughts continued. 'He would be gutted'. Samantha made her way down the stairs; she very gently and carefully took all six chicks out of the nest. Returning to her bedroom she slowly cut all the birds open with a knife. While she killed the chicks she felt pleased; felt elated; she felt powerful; she was hurting her dad. 'He will be gutted' she relished the thought. After the dreadful deed had been completed she was overwhelmed by shame, and self disgust For years Steve had spoken to her on many occasions. She could not stand to hear what he had to say. She hated what he was saying. At times she despised him for the things he said. But when she faced death, she knew of only one person to turn to.

THE SATANIC REBELLION

And the Heavenly Realms

S C SAYLES

PUBLISHED BY EVOLSIAY TULIP

Why Did Satan Rebel Against A Holy God?

Hebrews 1:1-13 (KJV)

1 God, who at sundry times and in divers manners spake in time past unto the fathers by the prophets,

2 Hath in these last days spoken unto us by his Son, whom he hath appointed heir of all things, by whom also he made the worlds;

3 Who being the brightness of his glory, and the express image of his person, and upholding all things by the word of his power, when he had by himself purged our sins, sat down on the right hand of the Majesty on high:

4 Being made so much better than the angels, as he hath by inheritance obtained a more excellent name than they.

5 For unto which of the angels said he at any time, Thou art my Son, this day have I begotten thee? And again, I will be to him a Father, and he shall be to me a Son?

6 And again, when he bringeth in the firstbegotten into the world, he saith, And let all the angels of God worship him.

7 And of the angels he saith, Who maketh his angels spirits, and his ministers a flame of fire.

8 But unto the Son he saith, Thy throne, O God, is for ever and ever: a sceptre of righteousness is the sceptre of thy kingdom.

9 Thou hast loved righteousness, and hated iniquity; therefore God, even thy God, hath anointed thee with the oil of gladness above thy fellows.

10 And, Thou, Lord, in the beginning hast laid the foundation of the earth; and the heavens are the works of thine hands:

11 They shall perish; but thou remainest; and they all shall wax old as doth a garment;

12 And as a vesture shalt thou fold them up, and they shall be changed: but thou art the same, and thy years shall not fail.

13 But to which of the angels said he at any time, Sit on my right hand, until I make thine enemies thy footstool?

Hebrews 9:11-24 (KJV)

11 But Christ being come an high priest of good things to come, by a greater and more perfect tabernacle, not made with hands, that is to say, not of this building;

12 Neither by the blood of goats and calves, but by his own blood he entered in once into the holy place, having obtained eternal redemption for us.

13 For if the blood of bulls and of goats, and the ashes of an heifer sprinkling the unclean, sanctifieth to the purifying of the flesh:

14 How much more shall the blood of Christ, who through the eternal Spirit offered himself without spot to God, purge your conscience from dead works to serve the living God?

15 And for this cause he is the mediator of the new testament, that by means of death, for the redemption of the transgressions that were under the first testament, they which are called might receive the promise of eternal inheritance.

16 For where a testament is, there must also of necessity be the death of the testator.

17 For a testament is of force after men are dead: otherwise it is of no strength at all while the testator liveth.

18 Whereupon neither the first testament was dedicated without blood.

19 For when Moses had spoken every precept to all the people according to the law, he took the blood of calves and of goats, with water, and scarlet wool, and hyssop, and sprinkled both the book, and all the people,

20 Saying, This is the blood of the testament which God hath enjoined unto you.

21 Moreover he sprinkled with blood both the tabernacle, and all the vessels of the ministry.

22 And almost all things are by the law purged with blood; and without shedding of blood is no remission.

23 It was therefore necessary that the patterns of things in the heavens should be purified with these; but the heavenly things themselves with better sacrifices than these.

24 For Christ is not entered into the holy places made with hands, which are the figures of the true; but into heaven itself, now to appear in the presence of God for us:

25 Nor yet that he should offer himself often, as the high priest entereth into the holy place every year with blood of others;

26 For then must he often have suffered since the foundation of the world: but now once in the end of the world hath he appeared to put away sin by the sacrifice of himself.

Job 1:1-6 (KJV)

1 There was a man in the land of Uz, whose name was Job; and that man was perfect and upright, and one that feared God, and eschewed evil.
2 And there were born unto him seven sons and three daughters.
3 His substance also was seven thousand sheep, and three thousand camels, and five hundred yoke of oxen, and five hundred she asses, and a very great household; so that this man was the greatest of all the men of the east.
4 And his sons went and feasted in their houses, every one his day; and sent and called for their three sisters to eat and to drink with them.
5 And it was so, when the days of their feasting were gone about, that Job sent and sanctified them, and rose up early in the morning, and offered burnt offerings according to the number of them all: for Job said, It may be that my sons have sinned, and cursed God in their hearts. Thus did Job continually.
6 Now there was a day when the sons of God came to present themselves before the Lord, and Satan came also among them.

The Adversary

The Book of Job is unmatched in the writings of the OT .Written about 1500 BC it is one of the oldest of all the Books of the Bible.
Satan plays a very relevant role in the book of Job. Although he is only mentioned at the very beginning. Satan is a subject that very few Christian know much about:-

"I only want to know about Jesus" , is often the refrain.

"Yes" – but Jesus wants us to know something about Satan" is the Biblical reply:-

This is a detective investigation, piecing together the Story of Satan:- and I believe there is a real blessing for us if we come to understand what has been happening behind the scenes .

Behind The Scenes

Behind the scenes is an apt term, for this is what we are given a glimpse of :-

In the opening Chapters of the book of Job;- the curtain is pulled back on the stage of life and we are given a glimpse behind the scenes.

1 There was a man in the land of Uz, whose name was Job; and that man was perfect and upright, and one that feared God, and eschewed evil.
2 And there were born unto him seven sons and three daughters.
3 His substance also was seven thousand sheep, and three thousand camels, and five hundred yoke of oxen, and five hundred she asses, and a very great household; so that this man was the greatest of all the men of the east.
4 And his sons went and feasted in their houses, every one his day; and sent and called for their three sisters to eat and to drink with them.
5 And it was so, when the days of their feasting were gone about, that Job sent and sanctified them, and rose up early in the morning, and offered burnt offerings according to the number of them all: for Job said, It may be that my sons have sinned, and cursed God in their hearts. Thus did Job continually.
6 Now there was a day when the sons of God came to present themselves before the Lord, and Satan came also among them.
7 And the Lord said unto Satan, Whence comest thou? Then Satan answered the Lord, and said, From going to and fro in the earth, and from walking up and down in it.
8 And the Lord said unto Satan, Hast thou considered my servant Job, that there is none like him in the earth, a perfect and an upright man, one that feareth God, and escheweth evil?
9 Then Satan answered the Lord, and said, Doth Job fear God for nought?

10 Hast not thou made an hedge about him, and about his house, and about all that he hath on every side? thou hast blessed the work of his hands, and his substance is increased in the land.

11 But put forth thine hand now, and touch all that he hath, and he will curse thee to thy face.

12 And the Lord said unto Satan, Behold, all that he hath is in thy power; only upon himself put not forth thine hand. So Satan went forth from the presence of the Lord. (KJV)

We are informed that one day the Sons of God came to present themselves to the LORD

This a subject of much confusion and dispute among scholars:- I humbly give you what I believe is the clear teaching of scripture on this matter.

Job 1:6

Now there was a day when the sons of God came to present themselves before the LORD, and Satan also came among them.

The sons of God in this verse refers to Angels, although not every Bible scholar would agree, but as you will see the context sets the text for us.

The Father in Heaven as Three types of "sons"

1/The Only Begotten Son – The Eternal Son- The Second person of the Trinity – Jesus Christ:-

John 1:18

No one has seen God at any time. The only begotten Son, who is in the bosom of the Father, He has declared Him.

2/ The created sons – The Angels – as referred to here in our text. And elsewhere in scripture for example

Job 38:7

When the morning stars sang together, And all the sons of God shouted for joy?

3/ The adopted Sons

Galatians 3:26

For you are all sons of God through faith in Christ Jesus.

Romans 8:15 (NKJV)

For you did not receive the spirit of bondage again to fear, but you received the Spirit of adoption by whom we cry out, "Abba, Father."

Ephes. 1:5 (NKJV)

having predestined us to adoption as sons by Jesus Christ to Himself, according to the good pleasure of His will,

As always the context of the verse in question informs us of whom the text is speaking:-

In the Job passage it is obvious that supernatural beings are in view, the sons of God present themselves to God, and Satan was with them.

Rev. 12:9
So the great dragon was cast out, that serpent of old, called the Devil and Satan, who deceives the whole world;

Satan is an evil spirit creature, the old serpent, the devil, who is a bitter enemy to men, especially to Christ and his people;

The name as so often in scripture reveals something of the nature, something of the character. Satan hates God's people and his opposition to them manifests this hatred:

The name Satan means, "an adversary", "an apostate" or "an accuser".

It was with respect to Job that this being known as Satan makes himself known, and therefore. Satan came with an intent to contradict what the "Sons of God" should say of him, and to accuse Job before God;

He came among the Sons of God as one of them, or he came, being sent for, and to give an account of himself, and of what he had been doing in the world.

We pause at this point to ponder some questions.

Where did Satan come from originally, when was he created?

Genesis 1:1

In the beginning God created the heavens and the earth.

Genesis 1:31

Then God saw everything that He had made, and indeed it was very good. So the evening and the morning were the sixth day.

God saw all that he had created, and indeed it was good:-

Gad saw "all". The use of the term is "universal". God saw everthying He had created and it was good. "What was Good? All that he had created.

No evil as of yet existed.

On the six day evil did not exist :-

Yet by Genesis chapter 3 the devil is at work:-

Genesis 3:1 Now the serpent was more cunning than any beast of the field which the LORD God had made. And he said to the woman, "Has God indeed said, 'You shall not eat of every tree of the garden'?"

And we know from REV 12 the following.

Rev 12 tell us that the serpent in this passage is the Devil – Satan- "that serpent of old, called the Devil and Satan"

When had The devil been created ? after the sixth day? What of the angels when were they created?

Psalm 148:2-5
Praise Him, all His angels;
Praise Him, all His hosts!
[3] Praise Him, sun and moon;
Praise Him, all you stars of light!
[4] Praise Him, you heavens of heavens,
And you waters above the heavens!
[5] Let them praise the name of the LORD,
For He commanded and they were created.

Genesis 2:1 (NKJV)

Thus the heavens and the earth, and all the host of them, were finished.

Sometimes in Scripture we have an incident when a person is addressed :- but Satan himself is the one whom is operating behind the scenes and he is also addressed:-

We see this in the case of Simon Peter (Mt 16)

Jesus had been telling Peter how blessed he was that the Father had revealed to him, Jesus's identity as the Son of God.

Peter then tried to rebuke Jesus for speaking of his death. Jesus turns to Peter but speaks to the Supernatural being behind the scenes.

Matthew 16:22-23

(22)Then Peter took Him aside and began to rebuke Him, saying, "Far be it from You, Lord; this shall not happen to You!"

(23) But He turned and said to Peter, "Get behind Me, Satan! You are an offense to Me, for you are not mindful of the things of God, but the things of men."

This is happens a number of times in Scripture and will help us in our inquire:-

The Prophet Isaiah speaking against the king of Babylon, suddenly turns his address to the angel Lucifer behind the Scenes .

Isaiah 14:12-14
(12) "How you are fallen from heaven,
O Lucifer, son of the morning!
How you are cut down to the ground,
You who weakened the nations!
[13] For you have said in your heart:
'I will ascend into heaven,

I will exalt my throne above the stars of God;

I will also sit on the mount of the congregation

On the farthest sides of the north;

[14] I will ascend above the heights of the clouds,

I will be like the Most High.'

Oh Lucifer , son of the morning. This signifies his outshining of the other stars, (as the morning star outshines the rest).

Satan before his fall was the chief angel, the brightest of all the stars in Heaven. The angels are often called the stars of heaven.

Job 38:7

When the morning stars sang together, And all the sons of God shouted for joy?

Rev. 12:3-4 And another sign appeared in heaven: behold, a great, fiery red dragon having seven heads and ten horns, and seven diadems on his heads. [4] His tail drew a third of the stars of heaven and threw them to the earth. And the dragon stood before the woman who was ready to give birth, to devour her Child as soon as it was born.

Elsewhere in Scripture we have another example. Ezekiel speaking to the king of Tyre, likewise speaks to the agent behind the scenes.

Ezekiel 28:12-19

"Son of man, take up a lamentation for the king of Tyre, and say to him, 'Thus says the Lord GOD:

"You were the seal of perfection,

Full of wisdom and perfect in beauty.

[13] You were in Eden, the garden of God;

Every precious stone was your covering:

The sardius, topaz, and diamond,

Beryl, onyx, and jasper,

Sapphire, turquoise, and emerald with gold.

The workmanship of your timbrels and pipes

Was prepared for you on the day you were created.

[14] "You were the anointed cherub who covers;

I established you;

You were on the holy mountain of God;

You walked back and forth in the midst of fiery stones.

[15] You were perfect in your ways from the day you were

created, Till iniquity was found in you.

[16] "By the abundance of your trading

You became filled with violence within,

And you sinned;

Therefore I cast you as a profane thing

Out of the mountain of God;

And I destroyed you, O covering cherub,

From the midst of the fiery stones.

[17] "Your heart was lifted up because of your beauty;

You corrupted your wisdom for the sake of your splendor;

I cast you to the ground,

I laid you before kings,

That they might gaze at you.

[18] "You defiled your sanctuaries

By the multitude of your iniquities,

By the iniquity of your trading;

Therefore I brought fire from your midst;

It devoured you,

And I turned you to ashes upon the earth

In the sight of all who saw you.

[19] All who knew you among the peoples are astonished at you;

You have become a horror,

And shall be no more forever."

In this very revealing portion of scripture, we learn that this Cherub or angel was once filled with wisdom and perfect beauty. He is referred to as being perfect in his ways, from the day he was created until iniquity was found in him V 15

V17 "Your heart was lifted up because of your beauty;
You corrupted your wisdom for the sake of your splendor;

We are starting to get a picture now of the unfolding of events behind the scenes. But we have many questions unanswered. Some of the references in the Ezekiel passages that we have read could well be speaking of future events (ie of him being destroyed by fire V18)

Matthew 25:41

Then He will also say to those on the left hand, 'Depart from Me, you cursed, into the everlasting fire prepared for the devil and his angels:

24

Could the fire of Ezekial 28:18 be pointing towards the final destruction of the Devil?

The Mathew Passage tells us that Satan was not alone when he fell. Rev 12 helps us again at this point:-

Rev. 12:7-9
And war broke out in heaven: Michael and his angels fought with the dragon; and the dragon and his angels fought, [8] but they did not prevail, nor was a place found for them in heaven any longer. [9] So the great dragon was cast out, that serpent of old, called the Devil and Satan, who deceives the whole world; he was cast to the earth, and his angels were cast out with him.

Verse 3-4 of the same chapter tell us the number of Angels who fell with Lucifer;

Rev. 12:3-4

And another sign appeared in heaven: behold, a great, fiery red dragon having seven heads and ten horns, and seven diadems on his heads. [4] His tail drew a third of the stars of heaven and threw them to the earth. ....

Because of his pride, Lucifer sinned.Why the hatred towards humankind and Jesus and his people in particular?

Notice in Ezekiel that the Devil is referred to as the "anointed" cherub who covers or guardian cherub as some translate the term.

Ezekiel 28:14

"You were the anointed cherub who covers;
I established you;

He is called the anointed cherub .

This expression alone shows him to have sat higher than any other cherub: for his being anointed, must signify his being distinguished from the others.

Anointing of old was used as a note of distinction , to show that a person was marked out from all the rest.

"Who Covers"

He is called the cherub who covers:-

There is a reference to the covering cherubs in the temple , the holy of holies. Next to the throne of God.

Exodus 25:20-22

And the cherubim shall stretch out their wings above, covering the mercy seat with their wings, and they shall face one another; the faces of the cherubim shall be toward the mercy seat. [21] You shall put the mercy seat on top of the ark, and in the ark you shall put the Testimony that I will give you. [22] And there I will meet with you, and I will speak with you from above the mercy seat, from between the two cherubim which are on the ark of the Testimony, about everything which I will give you in commandment to the children of Israel.

From this it appears, that by the covering cherub is meant the cherub next to the throne of God having a high a place in the Holy of Holies.

In the Temple in the Holy of Holies, there were two cherubim that covered the mercy-seat in the temple.

And from our earlier passage in Hebrews 9:11-24 , we know the temple is a copy (a picture or ullustration) of the Heavenlies

Hebrews 9:2-5

For a tabernacle was prepared: the first part, in which was the lampstand, the table, and the showbread, which is called the sanctuary; [3] and behind the second veil, the part of the tabernacle which is called the Holiest of All, [4] which had the golden censer and the ark of the covenant overlaid on all sides with gold, in which were the golden pot that had the manna, Aaron's rod that budded, and the tablets of the covenant; [5] and above it were the cherubim of glory overshadowing the mercy seat. Of these things we cannot now speak in detail.

And notice verse Hebrews 9:23 (NKJV)

Therefore it was necessary that the copies of the things in the heavens should be purified with these......,

The temple was a copy, a type, a symbolic type of the actual heavenly things.

Before his fall ,

Lucifer is spoken of as being, the one entitled to this great honour. Next to the Throne of God.The anointed cherub.

It should be noted that the word translated "cover" often commonly signifies "protect" to cover something is to protect or guard it.

We have all the evidence before us;- all the ingredients of the fall.

But was the spark that ignited the fall, what was the catalyst that occasioned the fall? We know that the wicked spirits know something of the will of God. They have a limited knowledge of the things of God

Matthew 8:28-29
"When He had come to the other side, to the country of the Gergesenes, there met Him two demon-possessed men, coming out of the tombs, exceedingly fierce, so that no one could pass that way. [29] And suddenly they cried out, saying, "What have we to do with You, Jesus, You Son of God? Have You come here to torment us before the time?"

The Demons and evil angels, know that they will be sent to Hell! They know something of the work of Christ.

Rev. 12:12
Therefore rejoice, O heavens, and you who dwell in them! Woe to the inhabitants of the earth and the sea! For the devil has come down to you, having great wrath, because he knows that he has a short time."

But the Angels both Holy and Fallen do not know all of the mystery of the Gospel.

1 Peter 1:10-12

Of this salvation the prophets have inquired and searched carefully, who prophesied of the grace that would come to you, [11] searching what, or what manner of time, the Spirit of Christ who was in them was indicating when He testified beforehand the sufferings of Christ and the glories that would follow. [12] To them it was revealed that, not to themselves, but to us they were ministering the things which now have been reported to you through those who have preached the gospel to you by the Holy Spirit sent from heaven--things which angels desire to look into.

The Angels had a limited understanding of the Gospel:- Yet they knew something of the plan of God:-

Now lets put it all together:-

Lucifer, the anointed covering Cherub. Anointed above all other angels.Created perfect in his ways. The highest of all the Angels. He was there in the Garden of God. When God created man. Man created lower than the angels

Hebrews 2:6-7 (NKJV)

But one testified in a certain place, saying:

"What is man that You are mindful of him,

Or the son of man that You take care of him?

[7] You have made him a little lower than the angels;

You have crowned him with glory and honor,

And set him over the works of Your hands.

God tells the Angels something of his plan for mankind and for the Angels:-

He tells them about a man. About one man in Particular.
Of whom it is written. Of whom it was said. This man. This Human being

Hebrews 1:5-9 (NKJV)

For to which of the angels did He ever say:
"You are My Son,
Today I have begotten You"?
And again:
"I will be to Him a Father,
And He shall be to Me a Son"?
[6] But when He again brings the firstborn into the world, He says:
"Let all the angels of God worship Him."
[7] And of the angels He says:
"Who makes His angels spirits
And His ministers a flame of fire."

[8] But to the Son He says:
"Your throne, O God, is forever and ever;
A scepter of righteousness is the scepter of Your Kingdom.
[9] You have loved righteousness and hated lawlessness;
Therefore God, Your God, has anointed You
With the oil of gladness more than Your companions."

Speaking of a man, a human being created a little lower than the angels. Almighty God the commands

"Let all the angels of God worship Him'

Let all the angels of God worship a man!

The verse has a universal term "all" (everyone of them without exception)

"Let all the angels of God worship Him'

Lucifer was informed that he would bow the knee to one of these humans:!

This was the catalyst. Lucifer could not bear it, he anointed cherub, with all his beauty.Having to bow to a man, His pride would not allow it.

Jonathan Edwards probably the greatest American Philosopher and a giant of a Theologian, on this very subject wrote concerning Lucifer

" But when it was revealed to him , that he must be a ministering spirit to the race of mankind which he had seen newly created, which appeared so feeble, mean, and despicable, so vastly inferior, not only to him, the prince of the angels ...but also to the inferior angles, and that he must be subject to one of that race that should hereafter be born, he could not bear it. This occasioned his fall: and now he and the other angels that he drew away with him are fallen"

Dr Goodwin writes

" A lower degree of accursed pride fell into the heart of the devil himself whose sin in first apostatizing from God; is conceived to be a stomaching that man should one day be advanced unto the hypostatitical union, and be one person with the Son of God"

The Angels were told something of the wonders of Christ, that one day a man would share the throne of Heaven and all the angels would worship him.

That one particular human was to be the head of all creation, the head of all principality and powers. The King of Kings. As a consequence the angels and men should have their grace from him.

This kingdom was rejected by many of the angels , and they refused to be subject to the Christ, and in opposition to this they set up another kingdom and made war with mankind, and drew humanity into the darkness of the kingdom of Satan.

Very briefly I will touch on the Angels who did not fall, for it needs to be said.

The reason that they did not fall:-

They resisted a great temptation.

The resisted Lucifer the ringleader, while many of their multitude rebelled.

A war in Heaven.Heaven divided. Heaven spoiled.

The angels that did not fall: stood by grace, by the grace of God:-

1 Tim. 5:21
I charge you before God and the Lord Jesus Christ and the elect angels .....

The angels that did not fall were elect: by the grace of God they stood, By the grace of God they withstood the temptation to rebel.

Suffice to say that in Heaven humility is a position of authority :- If you want to be great in Heaven you have to be least, you have to serve.

Lucifer fell because of his pride,he refused to bow to a man,the son of man:-

The elect angels humbled themselves in submission to the will of God:- so in a mysterious way the holy angles owe their heavenly security to The Man Jesus Christ.

Not as saviour but as their LORD. So we have the war, the rebellion in Heaven.The fall of Satan and his angels, and thereafter the fall of mankind.

The Bible teaches that Lucifer, Satan the Devil did not lose his place in heaven when he fell into rebellion. For he was still the anointed covering Cherub, although he was at war.

His original position as the anointed cherub explains much to us :-

Remember what we said earlier about Lucifer. **He is called the anointed cherub .**

This expression alone shows him to have sat higher than any other cherub: for his being anointed, must signify his being distinguished from the others. Anointing of old was used as a note of distinction , to show that a person was marked out from all the rest.

Who Covers

He is called the cherub who covers. Remember the reference to the covering cherubs in the temple, the holy of holies. Next to the throne of God.

Lucifer has become Satan .He is next to the Throne of God – he has access to the Throne of God:-

Job 1:6

Now there was a day when the sons of God came to present themselves before the LORD, and Satan also came among them.

What does Satan say? Does he agree with God when he is questioned concerning the righteousness of Job? No he accuses Job to God. He slates him , Slanders him. The Name Satan means adversary or accuser

Rev. 12:
....for the accuser of our brethren, who accused them before our God day and night,

It has to be accusing them Before the throne of God.

Rev. 12:10-12 (NKJV)

Then I heard a loud voice saying in heaven, "Now salvation, and strength, and the kingdom of our God, and the power of His Christ have come, for the accuser of our brethren, who accused them before our God day and night, has been cast down. [11] And they overcame him by the blood of the Lamb and by the word of their testimony, and they did not love their lives to the death. [12] Therefore rejoice, O heavens, and you who dwell in them! Woe to the inhabitants of the earth and the sea! For the devil has come down to you, having great wrath, because he knows that he has a short time."

In this passage the accuser is cast down out of heaven:- but this is after he has accused the brethren day and night, not before ,

For he became the accuser, the accuser near the throne of God, accusing day & night (before he was cast out of heaven).

Something happened, the text makes it very clear:-

Rev. 12:7-11
And war broke out in heaven: Michael and his angels fought with the dragon; and the dragon and his angels fought, [8] but they did not prevail, nor was a place found for them in heaven any longer. [9] So the great dragon was cast out, that serpent of old, called the Devil and Satan, who deceives the whole world; he was cast to the earth, and his angels were cast out with him.
[10] Then I heard a loud voice saying in heaven, "Now salvation, and strength, and the kingdom of our God, and the power of His Christ have come, for the accuser of our brethren, who accused them before our God day and night, has been cast down. [11] And they overcame him by the blood of the Lamb and by the word of their testimony, and they did not love their lives to the death.

The "they" must refer to the ones accused and the "overcoming" of the "they", somehow aided Michael in his fight.

Satan lost his heavenly place not when he fell into rebellion. Many people are confused with the term "fall". A fall from grace or fall from heaven? If a text speaks of being cast out . When there is no chronological marker. It could be speaking of a future event (as we have seen.) Plus there is a difference between a "fall" and being "cast out". Satan was in heaven at the time of Job and afterwards accusing the people of God to the face of God;-

He was the anointed cherub next to the throne. God had to answer the accusations of the enemy of Christ and his people.

36

Satan although the father of lies, would have been accusing God's people of their sins. One verse that does cause some peole a problem as to when Satan lost his place in Heaven is.

Luke 10:18
And He said to them, "I saw Satan fall like lightning from heaven.

The context of the verse, is not concerned with casting out of heaven but with the fall of Satan's kingdom. This interpretation fits the context and the fall was so obvious Jesus compared it to lightning.

Satan's Kingdom was falling, the demons were subject to the disciples as they ministered in the name of Christ. The fall of Satan's kingdom was as obvious as lighting falling from heaven. All sound commentaries take this position.

When did Satan lose his heavenly position? and how?

The answer is found in the Hebrews passage we read earlier

Hebrews 9:11-24

But Christ came as High Priest of the good things to come, with the greater and more perfect tabernacle not made with hands, that is, not of this creation. [12] Not with the blood of goats and calves, but with His own blood He entered the Most Holy Place once for all, having obtained eternal redemption. [13] For if the blood of bulls and goats and the ashes of a heifer, sprinkling the unclean, sanctifies for the purifying of the flesh, [14] how much more shall the blood of Christ, who through the eternal Spirit offered Himself without spot to God, cleanse your conscience from dead works to serve the living God? [15] And for this reason He is the Mediator of the new covenant, by means of death, for the redemption of the transgressions under the first covenant, that those who are called may receive the promise of the eternal inheritance.

[16] For where there is a testament, there must also of necessity be the death of the testator. [17] For a testament is in force after men are dead, since it has no power at all while the testator lives. [18] Therefore not even the first covenant was dedicated without blood. [19] For when Moses had spoken every precept to all the people according to the law, he took the blood of calves and goats, with water, scarlet wool, and hyssop, and sprinkled both the book itself and all the people, [20] saying, "This is the blood of the covenant which God has commanded you." [21] Then likewise

he sprinkled with blood both the tabernacle and all the vessels of the ministry. [22] And according to the law almost all things are purified with blood, and without shedding of blood there is no remission.

[23] Therefore it was necessary that the copies of the things in the heavens should be purified with these, but the heavenly things themselves with better sacrifices than these. [24] For Christ has not entered the holy places made with hands, which are copies of the true, but into heaven itself, now to appear in the presence of God for us;

Did you catch the last two verses and their significance to our study?

v23 Therefore it was necessary that the copies of the things in the heavens should be purified with these, but the heavenly things themselves with better sacrifices than these. [24] For Christ has not entered the holy places made with hands, which are copies of the true, but into heaven itself, now to appear in the presence of God for us;but the heavenly things themselves are purified , cleansed with better sacrifices than these.

notice this verse:

'but the heavenly things themselves are purified , cleansed'

Jesus's Blood in someway cleansed heaven.

The death of Christ not only brought salvation to sinners. but Heaven too was purified, cleansed of evil, cleansed of a sinful angel and his hordes. Does it all start to make sense now?

Rev. 12:10-12

Then I heard a loud voice saying in heaven, "Now salvation, and strength, and the kingdom of our God, and the power of His Christ have come, for the accuser of our brethren, who accused them before our God day and night, has been cast down. [11] And they overcame him by the blood of the Lamb and by the word of their testimony, and they did not love their lives to the death. [12] Therefore rejoice, O heavens, and you who dwell in them! Woe to the inhabitants of the earth and the sea! For the devil has come down to you, having great wrath, because he knows that he has a short time."

John 12:27-31

"Now My soul is troubled, and what shall I say? 'Father, save Me from this hour'? But for this purpose I came to this hour. [28] Father, glorify Your name." Then a voice came from heaven, saying, "I have both glorified it and will glorify it again." [29] Therefore the people who stood by and heard it said that it had thundered. Others said, "An angel has spoken to Him." [30] Jesus answered and said, "This voice did not come because of Me, but for your sake. [31] **Now is the judgment of this world; now the ruler of this world will be cast out.**

Cast out of where? Not the earth not yet, it must have been heaven as our texts suggests. We have a chronological marker "now".

The death of Christ Finished Satan in Heaven forever, he is no longer the anointed Cherub, he no longer has access to the throne of God. He no longer accuses the people of God before God. He can not bring a charge against the elect to God

Romans 8:33 - Who shall bring a charge against God's elect? It is God who justifies.

We have an amazing truth a great parralism. A beautiful Poetic Truth of God. The word anointed is radically the same Hebrew as the word Messiah. So in this respect Jesus is exalted into and above Lucifer's original place in Heaven. The anointed cherub has been replaced, by an anointed human being. Not one who stands next to the throne of God, but one who sits on the throne of God.

We said that the word to cover signifies to protect. Lucifer failed, he would not humble himself and bow the knee to a man, he would not humble himself to minister and protect a special race of humans.

This is the great reason the angels were created to serve God, and to minister to those who will be saved

Hebrews 1:13,14

But to which of the angels has He ever said:

"Sit at My right hand,

Till I make Your enemies Your footstool"?

[14] Are they not all ministering spirits sent forth to minister for those who will inherit salvation?

Would not his great work have been committed to the anointed cherub?

Jesus Christ the Son of God, the Son of Man is the great protector , he humbled himself even to the death on the cross. He defeated Satan first in the wilderness and finally on the cross :- Jesus the Messiah ,the anointed one , the protector and Saviour of elect man - gathers us as a hen gathers her chickens under her wing.

Satan is prowling the earth seeking to devour who he will.
Jesus is exalted far above principalities and powers. Satan can not accuse us before God, he has lost his heavenly place.

The anointed cherub has been replaced.We do not have an accuser standing next to the throne of God. We have a mediator, an advocate. Who even now is seated at the right hand of God, not accusing us, but interceding on our behalf.

1 John 2:1
We have an Advocate with the Father, Jesus Christ the righteous.

Hebrews 7:25
Therefore He is also able to save to the uttermost those who come to God through Him, since He always lives to make intercession for them.

Praise and thank God for Jesus Christ!

Alleluia.

THE NATURE OF HEAVEN

Is heaven Real?

What do we mean by Real?

Exist in reality, an actual place, a location.

The Bible refers to heaven about 550 times. The Hebrew word translated "heaven" (shamayim) is plural and literally means "the heights." "The aboves".

The Greek word translated "heaven" is "ouranos", which gave itself to the name of the planet Uranus. It refers to that which is raised up or lofty (Above).

Space / place / locality / realm. Lofty heights/ the above. Shamayim (plural)

Gen 1:1, 16, 2:1

Genesis 1:1
In the beginning God created the heavens and the earth.

Notice in this verse the heavsns is plural (more than one).

Three Heavens can be identified in Scripture

Genesis 1:6-10

Then God said, "Let there be a firmament in the midst of the waters, and let it divide the waters from the waters." [7] Thus God made the firmament, and divided the waters which were under the firmament from the waters which were above the firmament; and it was so. [8] And God called the firmament Heaven. So the evening and the morning were the second day.

(In the New International Version of the Bible, Godcalled the firmament "sky" The atmospheric heaven)

Sometimes when the Bible speaks of heaven, it is referring to the region usually the atmosphere around the earth. It's the air we breathe. For example,

Isaiah 55:9 says, "As the heavens are higher than the earth, so are My ways higher than your ways, and My thoughts than your thoughts. For as the rain and the snow come down from heaven ...."

Here the word "heaven" refers to the atmosphere, which is where the hydrological cycle occurs.

Psalm 147:8 says that God "covers the heavens with clouds."

So as we look out the window and to the heights, look above we, look to the heavens , what is the first heaven we see?

The Sky –This is the first heaven.

But if we look beyond the sky, look beyond the first heaven, what do we see? We see what we call outer-space(the outer-above).Where the planets and stars are situated.

Scripture also mentions this heaven. For example:

Genesis 1:14-16

"God said, Let there be lights in the expanse of the heavens.... God made the two great lights, the greater light to govern the day, and the lesser light to govern the night; He made the stars also. And God placed them in the expanse of the heavens to give light on the earth"

As we peer beyond the first height, the first Heaven we see the second heaven (outer space). Outer Space is is the second heaven.

2 Cor. 12:2 (NKJV)

I know a man in Christ who fourteen years ago--whether in the body I do not know, or whether out of the body I do not know, God knows--such a one was caught up to the third heaven.

In this passage. Paul says, "such a man (probably a reference to himself) was caught up to the third heaven". This verse clearly demonstrates there are three heavens (at least).

Why only three Heavens?

Some religions speak of seven (Seventh Heaven). We come across "three" many times in reality and within the universe. We wee it in the space-time relationship in the three dimensions that matter occupies in space. It is also seen in "time" as past, present and future. The universe has been created by a Triune Being. Three that is one.

The third heaven is the place where God dwells it is called his throne and Holy temple.

Psalm 11:4
The Lord is in His holy temple,
The Lord's throne is in heaven;
Isaiah 66:1
Thus says the Lord:
"Heaven is My throne,
And earth is My footstool.
Where is the house that you will build Me?
And where is the place of My rest?

Matthew 5:34
But I say to you, do not swear at all: neither by heaven, for it is God's throne;

Heaven is God's Throne. His Holy temple. Also in Heaven are the holy angels and those saints who now dwell there.

Rev. 5:11
Then I looked, and I heard the voice of many angels around the throne, the living creatures, and the elders; and the number of them was ten thousand times ten thousand, and thousands of thousands,

Rev. 7:9-11
After these things I looked, and behold, a great multitude which no one could number, of all nations, tribes, peoples, and tongues, standing before the throne and before the Lamb,

How Can an Omnipresent God Live in Heaven?

And if God created the Heavens where did he dwell before then? And where is it ? is it beyond , above outer-space- ?

Acts 17:24-28
God, who made the world and everything in it, since He is Lord of heaven and earth, does not dwell in temples made with hands. [25] Nor is He worshiped with men's hands, as though He needed anything, since He gives to all life, breath, and all things. [26] And He has made from one blood every nation of men to dwell on all the face of the earth, and has determined their preappointed times and the boundaries of their dwellings, [27] so that they should seek the Lord, in the hope that they might grope for Him and find Him, though He is not far from each one of us; [28] for in Him we live and move and have our being, as also some of your own poets have said, 'For we are also His offspring.'

Col. 1:16
For by Him all things were created that are in heaven and that are on earth, visible and invisible, whether thrones or dominions or principalities or powers. All things were created through Him and for Him.

Ephes. 4:10
He who descended is also the One who ascended far above all the heavens, that He might fill all things.

In 1 Kings 8:27 Solomon prays,

"Heaven and the highest heaven (lit. "heaven of heavens) cannot contain Thee, how much less this house which I have built!"

There is a sense in which the heaven of heavens can't contain God, yet in another sense it is His dwelling place.

Isaiah 57:15 says, "Thus says the high and exalted One who lives forever, whose name is Holy, I dwell on a high and holy place." God has a real dwelling place.

Isaiah 63:15 identifies that place: "Look down from heaven, and see from Thy holy and glorious habitation."

Psalm 33:13-14 says, "The Lord looks from heaven; He sees all the sons of men; from His dwelling place He looks out."

Psalm 102: 19
For He looked down from the height of His sanctuary;
From heaven the Lord viewed the earth,

We have established from scripture that there is a place where God dwells, and that place is called heaven.

Christ repeatedly stressed that the Father is in heaven.

Matthew 5:16 He says, "Let your light shine before men in such a way that they may see your good works, and glorify your Father who is in heaven."

Verse 45 says, "That you may be the sons of your Father who is in heaven."

In verse 38 Christ says, "I have come down from heaven."

In verses 41-42 He says, "I am the bread that came down out of heaven.... I have come down out of heaven."

In verses 50-51 He says, "This is the bread which comes down out of heaven, so that one may eat of it and not die. I am the living bread that came down out of heaven." Verse 58 says, "This is the bread which came down out of heaven."

Heaven is not a figment of the imagination, a feeling, or an emotion, it's a place, God's place.

It is a place, a location, a real dimension- a higher dimension. A spiritual dimension.

A heavenly, a spiritual dimension – the heavenlies
More substance than the physical realm – in that sense it is more solid.Explain – wispy spirit.

2 Cor. 4:18
while we do not look at the things which are seen, but at the things which are not seen. For the things which are seen are temporary, but the things which are not seen are eternal.

Spirits have more substance- are more solid than a brick/concrete wall – explain

The abode of such beings – spiritual , heavenly is more solid.
As we have bodies fit for the physical realm, made of the substance of this realm – a natural body for the natural realm

Heaven will be a new community of holiness and fellowship with God.
It will be a place of joy, peace, love, and fulfillment.
But we experience that partially even now.
The Holy Spirit is producing in us the fruit of "love, joy, peace, patience, kindness, goodness, faithfulness, gentleness, self-control"
Conclusion heaven is an actual place,
A real place.
The best of our spiritual experiences here is only a taste of heaven.
Our highest spiritual heights, profoundest depths, and greatest spiritual blessings will be normal in heaven.
Here on earth we are merely tasting the glories of the life to come.

To us heaven is now a sphere where we live under God's rule and His Spirit's blessing. Someday it will also be a place where we will walk in our glorified bodies.

John 17:24

Father, I desire that they also whom You gave Me may be with Me where I am, that they may behold My glory which You have given Me; for You loved Me before the foundation of the world.

In John 14:1 Christ says to His disciples, "Let not your heart be troubled; believe in God, believe also in Me. In My Father's house are many dwelling places; if it were not so, I would have told you; for I go to prepare a place for you. And if I go and prepare a place for you, I will come again, and receive you to Myself; that where I am, there you may be also."

Jesus is preparing a place where we will live in a glorified, spiritual yet solid form similar to that of the resurrected body of Christ. He walked, ate, and sang, but He also ascended through space into the third heaven.

We are longing for "the city which has foundations, whose architect and builder is God" (Heb. 11:10).

In ancient times a city was a place of safety and refuge. The nomadic people of those times were especially vulnerable to robbers, thieves, and the elements. Imagine after many weeks or even months of such wandering how refreshing it was to enter the protection of a walled city.

Every Christian needs to see himself as a pilgrim, wandering through this world, looking for "the city...whose architect and builder is God"--a real place where we will live with Christ. We will be with Him, just as the disciples were with Him after His resurrection.

Like Thomas, we will touch Him. We will sit with Him and sing with Him. The joy we have of walking with Christ and knowing that the Spirit lives within us is the pledge that someday we will live in heaven. If you are a Christian, the moment you leave this life you go to heaven. Paul said he preferred "to be absent from the body and to be at home with the Lord" (2 Cor. 5:8).

He said he desired "to depart and be with Christ" (Phil. 1:23).

When we consider that Christ prayed that all who know Him would spend eternity with Him (John 17:24), our hearts should overflow with gratitude.

We need to have the heart of Paul--yearning to to be clothed with our heavenly form and to exchange this transient world for eternal joy.

But I this lesson – I have to warn you all that heaven, is not for everyone.

By that I mean , the teaching of the Bible is that not everyone will be going to Heaven.

Matthew 7:21-23

"Not everyone who says to Me, 'Lord, Lord,' shall enter the kingdom of heaven, but he who does the will of My Father in heaven. [22] Many will say to Me in that day, 'Lord, Lord, have we not prophesied in Your name, cast out demons in Your name, and done many wonders in Your name?' [23] And then I will declare to them, 'I never knew you; depart from Me, you who practice lawlessness!'

Rev. 20:12

And I saw the dead, small and great, standing before God, and books were opened. And another book was opened, which is the Book of Life. And the dead were judged according to their works, by the things which were written in the books.

And anyone not found written in the Book of Life was cast into the lake of fire.

Heaven is tied up with Eternal life – or everlasting life.

John 17:3

And this is eternal life, that they may know You, the only true God, and Jesus Christ whom You have sent.

Getting into Heaven is very much like getting a Job, it not so much what you know, but who you know.

2And then I will declare to them, 'I never knew you; depart from Me"

My question to you this morning before I close

Is do you know Jesus Christ- are you saved, are you born again of the Holy Spirit.

How do you come to know Christ- How do you come to know God

If you believe this message- if you klnow that you are a sinner and deserve hell, and you dezsire God to forgive you , then seek

See him as the pearl of great price , and seek him

Seek him. seek after him.

Deut. 4:29

..seek the Lord your God, and you will find Him if you seek Him with all your heart and with all your soul.

1 Chron. 16:10-11

Glory in His holy name;
Let the hearts of those rejoice who seek the Lord!
[11] Seek the Lord and His strength;
Seek His face evermore!
Psalm 9:10
And those who know Your name will put their trust in You;
For You, Lord, have not forsaken those who seek You.
Psalm 14:2
The Lord looks down from heaven upon the children of men,
To see if there are any who understand, who seek God.
Proverbs 8:17
I love those who love me,
And those who seek me diligently will find me.
Jeremiah 29:13
And you will seek Me and find Me, when you search for Me with all
your heart.
Isaiah 55:6
Seek the Lord while He may be found,
Call upon Him while He is near.
Luke 11:9
"So I say to you, ask, and it will be given to you; seek, and you will find;
knock, and it will be opened to you.
Acts 17:27
so that they should seek the Lord, in the hope that they might grope
for Him and find Him, though He is not far from each one of us;
Hebrews 11:6
But without faith it is impossible to please Him, for he who comes to
God must believe that He is, and that He is a rewarder of those who
diligently seek Him.
When we seek God, with all our heart we shall find him
And we come to him for forgiveness of sin, now even now...
And later
we have Heaven to look forward to
Paul informs us
2 Cor. 5:1
For we know that if our earthly house, this tent, is destroyed, we have
a building from God, a house not made with hands, eternal in the
heavens.

We shall be exploring in next week in depth what the Apostle is actually saying-

Suffice at this point to conclude that by comparison with what we have, and know here, Heaven is beyond comparison.

Romans 8:18

.....not worthy to be compared ....

Its far to better,

I pray that God would comfort our hearts with his word this morning

Rev. 21:1-4

Now I saw a new heaven and a new earth, for the first heaven and the first earth had passed away. Also there was no more sea. [2] Then I, John, saw the holy city, New Jerusalem, coming down out of heaven from God, prepared as a bride adorned for her husband. [3] And I heard a loud voice from heaven saying, "Behold, the tabernacle of God is with men, and He will dwell with them, and they shall be His people. God Himself will be with them and be their God. [4] And God will wipe away every tear from their eyes; there shall be no more death, nor sorrow, nor crying. There shall be no more pain, for the former things have passed away."

Heaven part 2

John 3:12

If I have told you earthly things and you do not believe, how will you believe if I tell you heavenly things?

Over the next few weeks we shall be looking at the topic of Heaven and the Spiritual Realms

Heaven what it will be Like / what we will be like when we get there/ the New heaven. The spiritual realm and the nature of the spirit etc.

Is heaven Real?

What do we mean by Real

Exist in reality – an actual place

The Bible refers to heaven about 550 times. The Hebrew word translated "heaven" (shamayim) is plural and literally means "the heights." "The aboves"

The Greek word translated "heaven" is ouranos, which gave itself to the name of the planet Uranus. It refers to that which is raised up or lofty. Above.

Space / place / locality / realm. Lofty heights/ the above.

Shamayim (plural) Gen 1:1, 16, 2:1

Genesis 1:1

In the beginning God created the heavens and the earth.

Plural heavens – more than one.

3 Heavens can be identified in Scripture

The atmospheric heaven

The Sky –This is the first heaven.

But if we look beyond the sky- look beyond the first heaven, what do we see?

We see what we call outer-space- the outer-above- where the planets and stars are.

Outer Space –This is the second heaven.

2 Cor. 12:2 (NKJV)

I know a man in Christ who fourteen years ago--whether in the body I do not know, or whether out of the body I do not know, God knows--such a one was caught up to the third heaven.

In this passage

Paul says, "such a man [probably a reference to himself] was caught up to the third heaven" (emphasis added). That clearly demonstrates there are three heavens (at least).

{Digress / why only three ?}

The Jews had the concept of three heavens,

(But could there not be another ?)

The divine heaven

The third heaven is the place where God dwells it is called his throne and Holy temple

Isaiah 66:1

Thus says the Lord:

"Heaven is My throne,

And earth is My footstool.

Where is the house that you will build Me?

And where is the place of My rest?

Heaven is God's Throne- His Holy temple

How Can an Omnipresent God Live in Heaven?

And if God created the Heavens where did he dwell before then? And where is it ? is it beyond , above outer-space- ?

Acts 17: 28

.... for in Him we live and move and have our being, as also some of your own poets have said, 'For we are also His offspring.'

Ephes. 4:10

He who descended is also the One who ascended far above all the heavens, that He might fill all things.

There is a sense in which the heaven of heavens can't contain God, yet in another sense it is His dwelling place.

Explain -

1- where the birds fly

2- where the stars fly

3- where the angles fly-

His dwelling – although he is beyond

We have established from scripture that there is a place where God dwells, and that place is called heaven.

Heaven is not a figment of imagination, a feeling, or an emotion, it is a place, God's place.

2 Cor. 4:18

while we do not look at the things which are seen, but at the things which are not seen. For the things which are seen are temporary, but the things which are not seen are eternal.

Ephes. 3:10

to the intent that now the manifold wisdom of God might be made known by the church to the principalities and powers in the heavenly places,

Ephes. 6:12

For we do not wrestle against flesh and blood, but against principalities, against powers, against the rulers of the darkness of this age, against spiritual hosts of wickedness in the heavenly places.

Rev. 12:7-12 – Teaches that the dragon has been cast out of Heaven to earth. Where is he, where are the fallen angels, where are the demons? Where are the principalities, powers, and rulers of the darkness of this age, where are spiritual hosts of wickedness in the heavenly places if they are not in heaven but on earth?

They dwell in the spiritual places that are on the earth. They are the spiritual hosts of wickedness in the first spiritual dimension (first heaven) . We that are born of the Spirit, are seated above them in the third spiritual dimension (With Christ).

Ephes. 2:4-6
But God, who is rich in mercy, because of His great love with which He loved us, [5] even when we were dead in trespasses, made us alive together with Christ (by grace you have been saved), [6] and raised us up together, and made us sit together in the heavenly places in Christ Jesus,

Ephes. 1:3
Blessed be the God and Father of our Lord Jesus Christ, who has blessed us with every spiritual blessing in the heavenly places in Christ,

1 Cor. 2:14
But the natural man does not receive the things of the Spirit of God, for they are foolishness to him; nor can he know them, because they are spiritually discerned.

Matthew 4:17
From that time Jesus began to preach and to say, "Repent, for the kingdom of heaven is at hand."

Matthew 12:28
But if I cast out demons by the Spirit of God, surely the kingdom of God has come upon you.

John 3:3
Jesus answered and said to him, "Most assuredly, I say to you, unless one is born again, he cannot see the kingdom of God."

John 3:5
Jesus answered, "Most assuredly, I say to you, unless one is born of water and the Spirit, he cannot enter the kingdom of God.

Luke 17:20-21

Now when He was asked by the Pharisees when
the kingdom of God would come, He answered them and said,
"The kingdom of God does not come with observation; [21] nor will
they say, 'See here!' or 'See there!' For indeed, the kingdom of God is
within you."

John 5:24
"Most assuredly, I say to you, he who hears My word and believes in
Him who sent Me has everlasting life, and shall not come into
judgment, but has passed from death into life.

1 John 3:14
We know that we have passed from death to life,

Col. 1:13
He has delivered us from the power of darkness and conveyed us into
the kingdom of the Son of His love,

2 Cor. 5:17
Therefore, if anyone is in Christ, he is a new creation; old things have
passed away; behold, all things have become new.

1 John 5:11
And this is the testimony: that God has given us eternal life, and this
life is in His Son.

We are members of God's kingdom. Coming under his rule and
dominion.

My Spirit is in Christ, in the hevenly realm. My body is here in the
natural, but one day my body too will be redeemed. I'm alive in Christ.

Col. 3:3
For you died, and your life is hidden with Christ in God.

Col. 3:1-3
If then you were raised with Christ, seek those things which are above, where Christ is, sitting at the right hand of God. [2] Set your mind on things above, not on things on the earth. [3] For you died, and your life is hidden with Christ in God.

Can you not see? What has happened, a miracle. We look forward to the completion

1 Cor. 15:37-54
And what you sow, you do not sow that body that shall be, but mere grain--perhaps wheat or some other grain. [38] But God gives it a body as He pleases, and to each seed its own body. [39] All flesh is not the same flesh, but there is one kind of flesh of men, another flesh of animals, another of fish, and another of birds. [40] There are also celestial bodies and terrestrial bodies; but the glory of the celestial is one, and the glory of the terrestrial is another. [41] There is one glory of the sun, another glory of the moon, and another glory of the stars; for one star differs from another star in glory. [42] So also is the resurrection of the dead. The body is sown in corruption, it is raised in incorruption. [43] It is sown in dishonor, it is raised in glory. It is sown in weakness, it is raised in power. [44] It is sown a natural body, it is raised a spiritual body. There is a natural body, and there is a spiritual body. [45] And so it is written, "The first man Adam became a living being." The last Adam became a life-giving spirit. [46] However, the spiritual is not first, but the natural, and afterward the spiritual. [47] The first man was of the earth, made of dust; the second Man is the Lord from heaven. [48] As was the man of dust, so also are those who are made of dust; and as is the heavenly Man, so also are those who are heavenly. [49] And as we have borne the image of the man of dust, we shall also bear the image of the heavenly Man.
[50] Now this I say, brethren, that flesh and blood cannot inherit the kingdom of God; nor does corruption inherit incorruption. [51] Behold, I tell you a mystery: We shall not all sleep, but we shall all be changed-- [52] in a moment, in the twinkling of an eye, at the last trumpet. For the trumpet will sound, and the dead will be raised incorruptible, and we shall be changed. [53] For this corruptible must put on incorruption, and this mortal must put on immortality. [54] So

when this corruptible has put on incorruption, and this mortal has put on immortality, then shall be brought to pass the saying that is written: "Death is swallowed up in victory."

A Christian Philosophical Apologia

I must confess that a man is guilty of unpardonable arrogance who concludes, because an argument has escaped his own investigations, that therefore it does not really exist. (Hume; 1748; p 463)

The phenomenon that we have come to know as the paranormal is not new. Many identical stories and similar strange events can be found in all cultures and all ages.

The important thing to understand is that all paranormal activity is culturally interpreted.

A modern western interpretation is not exempt from this subjective bias. We live in the "space-age", we rather nicely have a space-age interpretation to explain the paranormal phenomena of the "alien" type. The interpretation is that we are not alone in the universe, other intelligent life-forms must exist, and in fact often visit and have dealings with humans.

The problem with cultural interpretation is that it is so difficult to be objective when looking at data. For our own personal interpretation , our own worldview gets in the way of us seeing the " true " picture.

Assumptions and presuppositions influence our interpretation of any logical reasoning, facts proofs etc, your worldview is bias, we always perceive reality through our tinted spectacles. The question is what is the truth? . Which interpretation is more in line with reality?

How do we assess the data, how do we scientifically prove our findings? Stephen Hawking the brilliant astrophysicist writes;

> Any physical theory is always provisional, in the sense that it is only a hypotheses: you can never prove it; (Hawking; 1995; p11).

~

We can not avoid relying upon the reports of people. We have to trust the reporters, unless they disqualify themselves by contradiction, error, lies etc.

The authority of an eye-witness is so powerful , that in court cases, their evidence must be either disproved, or the witness themselves must be discredited. In other words our trust / faith in the eye-witness or their report, must be removed.

Trust is exercised whenever, we read the report in the newspaper, the scientific paper, the things that our friends tell us, when we remember passed personal experiences. Even with our sensory perception, we exercise trust.

Trust is the prerequisite of all knowledge, and somewhere down the line there is an empirical foundation, be it an eye-witness account of an event, or something that we have experienced for ourselves.

We exercise trust, whenever we are dealing with knowledge, especially knowledge that is outside of our immediate experience. We give the greatest trust or authority to eye-witness accounts.

Dr Trueblood writes :

> Every proposition is really a judgment. When a man says "King Charles the First was executed" he means " I believe that King Charles the First was executed".
> Our dependence appears to be on facts but is really a dependence upon men.....most of what we believe about the external world is received second hand and rests on the prior belief that some men are more trustworthy reporters than others.....The conclusion to be reached ...is that we cannot avoid reliance upon some sort of authority. (Trueblood: 1987; p 67).

The earth is not being visited by extraterrestrial life-forms (physical beings from another planet etc.) But the earth is being " visited " by beings from a higher dimension ,that these visits have been going on for thousand of years and have been culturally interpreted .

The common denominators or " Trans-cultural markers" are noted and a conclusion is drawn that paint an all together different picture of what is really happening. When we strip away the cultural interpretation , strip away the veneer of understanding. By putting together that which transcends the culture , and is common to all the case studies , we then have a clearer picture of what is happening, a picture that is consistent with the Judeo-Christian worldview.

Higher dimension theory

We will use the concept of two-dimensional beings, used by Edwin A Abbott in 1884 (Abbott; 1998), Albert Einstein in chapter thirty-one of his theory of relativity (Einstein ;1961) And Dr Carl Sagan in his book Cosmos (Sagan; 1980; p 262).

Abbott, Einstein and Sagan used the concept of two-dimensional beings to illustrate the concept of non-Euclidean geometry. The pseudo-physics is used for analogy, even the most conventional of mainstream physicists resort to pseudo science in order assist thinking and develop hypotheses.

~

Imagine a strange universe where everyone is perfectly flat. This universe is called *"Flatverse"*. Some of the creatures are round, others are square, oblong, triangles, etc. Everyone in *Flatverse* has length and width, but no height whatever, they are all *"Flatties"*.
The Flatties know about left-right, and backward-forward. But have no concept, not a trace of comprehension about up (or down). If someone was to put forward a theory; mathematical, metaphysical etc. concerning *"UP "*, they would have no concept of it's direction . The *Flatties* would say to the person proposing the concept of "UP".

" Where is this strange dimension of which thee speaketh? "

The poor mathematician or metaphysician would not be able to point to it and would probably reply

" Why are you speaking oldy-worldy ? "

And try as he may he would never be able to show the direction of *"UP"*, even though according to his theory *"UP"* was actually everywhere and transcended their own Flatverse. For even the Flattie who put forward the theory could only have an intellectual understanding of "UP".

If a Flattie were to look in any direction , his perception of Flatverse would be that it was infinite. It went on for ever in all directions (two dimensions). But let us also imagine that the two-dimensional universe was actually warped around a third. Dimension.   In fact Flatverse was actually on the outside (or possibly inside) of a sphere. And the third dimensional world was inhabited by 3-dimensional beings. who exist in the third but have the ability to interact with the Flatverse.

What strange powers would these higher-dimensional beings have? They would be able to appear and disappear out of Flatverse at will. They would be able to travel between two points on the sphere via the third-dimension (thereby defying laws of two -dimensional travel etc.) They would be able to "see" inside the Flatties , and communicate directly with their minds, they would be Shapeshifters - having the ability to appear to the Flatties as anything they wanted to be. The higher-dimensional intelligence's (HDI) would have the ability to perform many strange things ; paranormal activities would fall into this classification of abilities.

Einstien etc. , then go onto suggest that it is possible that our Three-dimensional universe is in fact warped around an higher dimension; and although our universe appears to be endless , it is in fact limited. And no matter where you are in the universe , you are always exactly the same distance from its center. (the center being located in a higher-dimension) (all points on the surface of a ball , are the same distance from the center of the ball , the center of the ball being in a different dimension to the plane of the surface) .

~

The evidence from all types of paranormal activities, tend to support the theory that we are dealing with the same type of entities. From necromancy (communication with the dead) , spirit possession, close encounters of all kinds,(there is no basic difference between a medium "communicating " with a "dead" person, And a Channaler " communicating" with an "alien") and even some past life experiences, these and many other kinds of paranormal events can be recognized, and classified as HDI activity

The evidence shows that HDI's can communicate with humans more effectively when the human is in an ASC (trance, hypnotic, drug induced, astral projection. etc) . Most alien abduction experiences are pseudo-memories....

The British False Memory Society, (Bradford On Avon, Wiltshire BA15 1NA) have done much research into false memory syndrome and have a weight of evidence to collaborate their conclusions . Past life memories are pseudo-memories....It must be remembered that HDI have the ability to manipulate matter, (they could even appear themselves as a craft or anything they choose, to use a contemporary term ,HDI's are Shape-Shifters. All contact with aliens, spirits, " Dead " humans etc , is really contact with these HDI's (Who are Masquerading as aliens etc)

WHO? WHY?

Who are these beings?   What are they about?..............The beings have over the centuries gone by many names (cultural interpretation) and have appeared to humans in many forms......i.e........gods....spirits, demons, aliens, ascended masters, spirit guides, watchers, sons of God, Plaedians, Lyrans, Zeta Reticuli, Higherself , some have even appeared as The blessed Virgin Mary, and also appear as "ghosts" or spirits of dead humans etc. .

Why?.........Why do these beings appear under different guises.....why do they support cultural expectations.. why do they propagate many wordviews? Could it be that they have an hidden agenda...possibly to keep us from a correct worldview.if so why?

Higher-Dimensional physics informs us that the "Flatties" are bound by two dimensional physical laws. The Spirit and alien activity is consistent with HD physics. If the beings are not HDI they would behave in accordance with physical laws , the data for UFO, aliens, spirits, etc. points towards HDI and not physical entities. We are dealing with evidence
which points away from ETI towards HDI. But the most important thing is that you may have missed the whole point.

~

This blog is not really concerned with HDI or the paranormal but with presenting the Christian Worldview and an understanding of the paranormal is a consequence of the knowing the truth,

HOW TO KNOW THAT THE CHRISTIAN WORLDVIEW IS THE TRUTH.

Truth is that which corresponds to reality. We are dealing with a knowledge (a knowledge that the Christian worldveiw is true that is experimental and not just intellectual.)

An illustration dealing with the nature / types of knowledge will be helpful at this point.

Douglas Adams (Hitchhikers guide to the universe) writes a book. The book explains and teaches how humans can learn to fly. In which the art to unaided flying lies in the knack of falling to the ground and accidentally missing it.

A person reads the back of the book and says " What a load of rubbish ,humans can not fly, I'm not even going to waste my time in reading this silly book."

A second person comes along and says " I've got an open mind, and I have read the book, and it is indeed a load of rubbish. In fact I have written my own book disproving the belief that humans can fly".

A third person says "Well I also have read the book and I believe that it is true. Here is my book supporting my belief".

The second and third persons spend many a happy hour debating and arguing their respective beliefs on the issue.

For both hold valid points of view, based upon the same type of knowledge, but with different interpretations due to their own worldviews.

But a fourth person comes along . He reads the book and also believes it. And as a further act of faith , he puts into practice (or tests) what he has read and actually manages to fly.
The fourth persons knowledge is of a very different nature than the other three persons. This person has "proven" it to be true by experiment, he has experiential knowledge of the truth that he holds intellectually. (This is theory tested by experiment).

Although the third person holds the same intellectual truth , he does not know the truth experimentally.

The fourth person not only exercised trust to receive the truth in his head, but he also believed the truth in his "heart" which led him to action, where upon he came into experiential knowledge.

What this blog can tell you , you may grasp intellectually, you then could also believe it. But you can not know the truth experimentally. For how can we have an understanding of the higher-dimension when we are separated from it?.

We have seen how in the theory of the higher-Dimension it is all around us. This dimension is not physical, it can not be detected with physical instruments etc.   How can we have experiential knowledge of this dimension, how can we enter this dimension?

METAPHYSICAL ANTHROPOLOGY

(From the book "HIGHER DIMENSIONS & METAPHYSICAL ANTHROPOLOGY)

THE NATURE OF MAN , LIFE AND DEATH

What is life? Physical life is often defined by its biological attributes i.e. metabolism, reproduction, the ability to grow and respond to stimuli etc. But what of consciousness, and its relationship to physical life? We have physical life. we live, move and have our being in the physical universe. We are part of the physical universe. We are living physical beings and thus can function in the physical realm. Our physical life functions give us consciousness of the physical world, we can move, work (expend physical energy) , communicate and have relationships with other physical beings.

Is the human mind just a product of the brain? Does the human being have a soul? what is the soul?

> "The learned thinkers, scholars, sages, etc. Have used many words to describe the non-physical part of the makeup of man. In the traditional writings, the word mind is used less often than " reason" , " intellect" , " understanding", or "soul".
>
> There are other words such as "consciousness", "spirit", "psyche" which often carry some are part of the connotation of the word mind. Certain writers use the word " mind" as a synonym for one or more of these words and give it a meaning that other writers express in entirely exclusive terms." (Adler; 1990; p 140).

We have a difficulty in defining the non-physical part of mans nature. A common sense approach is best. Therefore in this blog, the word Soul is defined as " the non-physical part of man, the mind, the realm where thought, emotion, and memory are experienced."

We are only aware of our own ideas, our own perceptions, our own thoughts, all of our perceptions are "filtered" by our worldview. ....

The very fact that we have consciousness implies a being that is indeed conscious. Thus our self-knowledge is of a thinking , conscious substance. In other words we know our self first, and only by knowing this , do we know other things. Your mind must accept the fact , that because you have this knowledge of self, it implies an " Ego " that has it. The other things to be known outside of the self are / is "non-ego".

We can only know matter by having known Mind.

How do you know that you have a brain? By the valid testimony of anatomists as to the skulls of all humans (who are living). You only know your brain as an objective knowledge. Objective to that which knows. If you have an opinion about the brain, it is the instrument by which you think, not the "ego" who thinks. The mind / soul is a substance, that is not physical. The mind is conscious of the physical universe because it uses the brain as a type of interface (and the body as a vehicle.)

The human being is both physical and non-physical body and soul.

But what is death? Death is the cessation of life. The removal of life functions. Traditionally in many cultures the soul is believed to have left the body at the moment of physical death

It is the Soul that gives life to the body.

Probably the greatest definition of life, comes from the genius of John Owen (1616-86) who wrote that life was ;

" the act of a quickening principle on a subject to be quickened, by virtue of their union ". (Owen; 1981, Vol 3, p 283).

What Owen is saying is that the soul is the *quickening principle* (that which gives life) of the body (the body is the subject to be quickened).

Owen is stating that life is an act of the soul (*quickening principle)* on the body (*subject to be quickened,*) by virtue of the soul being in union with the body.

Therefore death is the separation of the quickening principle (soul) from the subject (body). When this happens the body is said to be dead.

Rather like an electric motor is said to be dead when separated from the electrical supply. The electrical energy is the quickening principle and the motor is the subject to be quickened.

At the moment of separation , the soul loses its consciousness of the physical, loses its interface (and its vehicle) with the physical realm, so it no longer has consciousness, it loses all of its life functions. But the soul still exists because it is non-physical.

Put another way. You have no consciousness of the higher-dimension. You know nothing of its nature, (just an intellectual theory). You are separated from (dead to) this higher realm. You are separated from the higher dimension.

As your soul gives life to your body . Your soul needs to be given higher-dimensional life. You have physical life, you do not have higher-dimensional life. (remember that death is separation and not non-existence). In other words your soul is dead.   It needs to be quickened by a quickening principle from the higher-dimension.

Let us return to " Flatverse". Remember the Two-dimensional " Flatties"? Let us further imagine that although the Flatties have flat bodies. This had not always been the case for their minds (souls). For the first Flatties where created (The first Flatties had minds (souls) that existed locally inside their bodies, but their souls (minds) where actually three-dimensional!

In effect, although they had two-dimensional (physical) life, they also had a three-dimensional life. Then a terrible thing happened to the Flatties, because of a foolish act, they lost the " higher -dimensional capacity " of their souls (minds). Thus becoming separated from the higher-dimension, they had higher-dimensionally died. Their minds had become flat (unspiritual or non- higher dimensional).

The consequence being, loss of all experimental knowledge of the higher realm, (loss of spiritual consciousness).

Imagine the Flatties scurrying about their daily business, they have lost all capacity in their minds (souls) for the higher-dimension. They have no awareness of the higher realm. But what would happen if some of the Flatties some how regained the three-dimensional life that their souls had lost? These Flatties would become conscious of the higher realm. They would have a different outlook on life. It would be impossible for them to convince a non-higher- dimensional Flattie, of the reality of what has happened to them (although friends and family would notice a change of behavior).

Remarkably in actual reality the blessed three-dimensional Flatties would be living to some degree in the higher realm.

Their bodies of course would still be two-dimensional with their souls in the body, but their souls also inhabit higher-dimensional space. In other words spiritually, the Flatties would exist to some degree in the higher realm, in the heavenly realms. (Ephesians 2:6).

Lets put it another way. You came into the physical universe by birth. How are you , flesh and blood, a physical being , ever going to become an higher-dimensional being ? ,By your own efforts? No its impossible, you need a quickening principle from the higher-dimension.

You need to be recreated as a higher-dimensional being, You need to be born into the higher –realm. Can this be done ?

This is what this whole book is concerned with. Ie to be higher-dimensional is to be in possession of the spiritual life.

SOME ANSWERS

Knowledge is possessed by exercising trust, we give the greatest authority to eye - witness accounts. What you are about to read you may grasp intellectually,

BUT YOU WILL NOT KNOW THE TRUTHS EXPERIMENTALLY UNLESS YOU EXERCISE "HEART" FAITH.

This essay can only help to uncover intellectual truths, to know the truths experimentally is an altogether more serious issue facing the reader, facing you. I only can point you towards gaining this Higher-Dimensional life.

There are HDI's who are active on the earth are propagating false worldviews; for the sole purpose of preventing humans from gaining this higher-dimensional life; but why?

Higher-Dimensional Beings

The most important point that we have looked at is to do with the make up of human nature. How that the mind/soul of humans is separated from (Dead to) the higher-dimension; and how because of this separation we have no awareness of the existence of such a dimension. But ;

When we looked at the metaphysical nature of death ie the .separation from the quickening principle. We said that humans need a quickening principle from the higher-dimension. How is this achieved?
What you are about to read you may grasp intellectually, but you will not know the truths experimentally unless you exercise trust (heart faith). You can not exercise this type of faith because your soul is dead to this higher-dimensional faith.

The higher-dimensions have been illustrated by the "Flatverse" picture. Another way of looking at the higher-realm. is to image the physical universe as a sponge; and then image that this sponge is submerged in water. The water fills the sponge , but it also transcends the sponge .

We now come to the HDI's many thousand of years ago a war broke out between the beings in the higher-dimension. This war took place in the area of water beyond the sponge. Tragically mankind was dragged into the conflict (the sponge area became part of the battle zone) and mankind became a causality of the war and as a result we lost our higher-dimensional life. Since that time though, a rescue mission has been launched to rescue us. (explain later).

Part of the consequence of our involvement is that we became "allies" with the wrong side, and it is this side that is trying to keep us from becoming higher-dimensional.

The battle is no longer taking place in the water beyond the sponge , it is taking place within the water in the sponge.

Image two circles that overlap (A Venn diagram) each circle represents a kingdom, the overlap area is the area of conflict (The sponge area).

We exist in this area of conflict. Our bodies are part of the "sponge realm", our souls are part of the "water realm" .

Our soul when we are born physically is dead, "or in darkness", i.e. separated from the quickening principle, because the quickening principle is at war with the kingdom in which our souls exist.

Our soul is in the kingdom of darkness. (The condition of death) But when we gain this new life, when we are born into the kingdom of light. We have changed sides; we have crossed over into life And as a result, we become aware of these truths experimentally . We become aware of the quickening principle.

MORE ANSWERS

We have been using terms that our modern space-age culture understands , terms like higher-dimensional. But this is just another way of saying spiritual. The Quickening Principle is the Holy Spirit. The rescue mission is the gospel of Jesus Christ to become an higher-dimensional; you must be born-again of the Spirit.

Faith is the prerequisite of all knowledge, and somewhere down the line there is an empirical foundation, be it an eye-witness account of an event, or something that we have experienced for ourselves. We exercise faith, whenever we are dealing with knowledge, especially knowledge that is outside of our immediate experience. We give the greatest trust or authority to eye-witness accounts)

COMPARE THESE WORDS

> Inasmuch as many have taken in hand to set in order a narrative of those things which have been fulfilled among us, just as those who from the beginning were eyewitnesses and ministers of the word delivered them to us, (Holy Bible; Luke 1:1-2).

> For we did not follow cunningly devised fables when we made known to you the power and coming of our Lord Jesus Christ, but were eyewitnesses of His majesty. (Holy Bible; 2 Peter 1:16).

These and many other passages in the Holy Bible give , or record eye-witness accounts, concerning Jesus and the things he did and said. Christians do not claim a blind faith in the Bible. God does not expect a blind faith, but a reasonable faith. There is more than enough evidence in the pages of scripture to prove it is truth.

Even so your worldview may not allow you to believe the gospel of Jesus Christ in spite of any evidence etc.

When the first man was created he was not a living being (or soul). The man's body was formed from the dust. But life came by virtue of the union with the Breath of God (Hebrew for Spirit is also the same for breath / wind (Hebrew is the original language)).

The Spirit of God is the "quickening principle". God himself is the " quickening principle" the man formed is the subject to be quickened.

".....the Lord God formed the man from the dust of the ground and breathed into his nostrils the breath of life, and the man became a living being. " (HOLY BIBLE , Genesis 2:7)

Life = " The act of a quickening principle on a subject to be quickened, by virtue of their union ".

Man became a living being, and thus could function in the physical realm (universe). His physical life functions gave him consciousness of the physical world , he could move, work, communicate and have fellowship with other physical creatures in the physical dimension.

But unlike the lesser creatures who had not been created in God's image (Holy Bible , Genesis 1:27) the first man had spiritual life, for he was created not with just a physical nature, but also a spiritual one. The spiritual nature is a capacity of the soul (mind), the souls life (spiritual life)

The man could communicate, and have fellowship with God. He would have been aware of God's presence (consciousness of God), he would have been able to do spiritual work etc.

God warned the first man not to eat from a certain tree

"...but you must not eat from the tree of knowledge of good and bad, for when you eat of it you will surely die" (Holy Bible, Genesis 3:17)

The Hebrew in that particular verse, literally means " dying you will die ". Which carries the concept of death being both an event and a process. The man was foolish and ate from the tree, the consequence being that he immediately died spiritually, and some time afterwards he died physically (event and process).

The Nature of Death

What is death?, earlier defined as the cessation of life. What actually happened to the first man?

If life is the act of union between a quickening principle and the subject to be quickened. Then death must be the separation of the quickening principle from the subject.

The Spirit of God removed himself from the soul of man , the effect being the death of the soul (event) / (spiritual death) the result was the loss of spiritual consciousness, etc.
The man's soul (or mind) lost its capacity for spiritual communion with God , he had lost all ability to function in the spiritual realm, lost all capability for experiential knowledge of the spiritual. He had lost consciousness of God.

The Spirit quickens the soul, as the soul quickens the body.

COMPARE THE WORDS OF JESUS:

> " Follow me and let the dead bury their own dead." (Holy Bible, Matthew 8:22)

Jesus was saying let the spiritually dead bury the physically dead. The cause of the separation from God (quickening principle) was the mans disobedience , or what the Bible calls sin. It is sin that has separated us from the Spirit.

Spiritual deadness, cessation of the spiritual life, separation from God, the condition of the unregenerate. All mankind are born into the world in this state. You my friend are spiritually dead. It is because of your *Spiritual Deadness* that you can not understand spiritual truth in any way but intellectually.

Rather like the Flatties , you have no experiential knowledge of the higher-dimension, at your best you may have a intellectual grasp (you may even believe intellectually). This leaves you in a very serious condition, do you fully appreciate the consequence of your state ?

THE STATE OF THE SPIRITUALLY DEAD

The Westminster Confession of Faith 1646 states in Chapter 9 section 3;

> " Man, by his fall into a state of sin, hath wholly lost all ability of will to any spiritual good accompanying salvation; so as a natural man, being altogether averse from good, and dead in sin, is not able by his own strength, to convert himself, or prepare himself thereunto" (Hodge; 1869; (1983) p161)

> "....the well known saying which has been borrowed from the writings of Augustine,
> that man's natural gifts were corrupted by sin, and his supernatural gifts withdrawn...........Hence it follows, that he is now an exile from the kingdom of God, so that all things that pertain to the blessed life of the soul are extinguished in him until he recovers them by the grace regeneration." (Calvin; 1845; (1990) p 115).

Jonathan Edwards (1703-58) theologian, and probably the greatest of all American Philosophers wrote these words;

> " As men come into the world, their natures are dreadfully depraved......
> .....It is awful to think that so excellent a creature as man is should be so ruined. The dreadfulness of the condition, which unconverted men are in in this respect, appears in the following things:
> .... God gave man a faculty of reason and understanding, which is a noble faculty. Herein he differs from all other creatures here below. He exalted in his nature above them, and is in this respect like the angels, and is made capable to know God, and to know spiritual and eternal things. And God gave him understanding for this end, that he might know him, and heavenly things, and made him capable to know these things as any others. But man has debased himself, and lost his glory in this respect. He has become ignorant of the excellency of God.........His understanding is full of darkness: his mind is blind, is altogether blind to spiritual things. Men are ignorant of God,

and of Christ........." (Edwards, 1834; Vol 2 , page 817)

The Bible teaches that the natural condition of mankind is that we are spiritually dead (or dead in sin). We cannot believe the gospel of Jesus Christ on any level but an intellectual one.

Because of this condition , it is impossible for us to be saved from spiritual death by any effort from ourselves. It is not possible for the dead to raise themselves to life. Why do you not believe?

> " The man without the Spirit does not accept the things that come from the Spirit of God, for they are foolishness to him, and he cannot understand them because they are spiritually discerned ." (Holy Bible, 1 Corinthians 2:14)

> " For the message of the cross is foolishness to those who are perishing, but to us who are being saved it is the power of God ." (Holy Bible , 1 Corinthians 1:14)

My friend , you can not, have not the power in and of yourself to believe. You can not convert yourself . You have not the spiritual capacity to understand spiritual truths, higher-dimensional truths, heavenly things.

> " I have spoken of earthly things and you do not believe; how then will you believe if I speak of heavenly things? (Jesus Christ, Holy Bible, John 3:12) .

Our physical birth gave us physical life only, to have spiritual life it is necessary for us to be regenerated spiritually, we need to be born of the Spirit of God.

> " Flesh gives birth to flesh, but the Spirit gives birth to spirit. You should not be surprised at my saying, "you should be born again." . (Jesus Christ, Holy Bible, John 3:6-7).

It was sin that caused the first humans to die spiritually and so all who are born from them are born spiritually dead, and the spiritual condition that we are in when we die physically is the condition that we will spend eternity in.

"Therefore, as through one man sin entered the world, and death through sin: and so death passed to all men..." (Holy bible, Romans 5:12)

Even though it is impossible for us to give spiritual life to ourselves, it is not impossible for God . The Born-again believer knows the following to be true:

" indeed, in our hearts we felt the sentence of death. But this happened that we might rely not on ourselves but on God, who raises the dead." (Holy Bible, 2 Corinthians 1:9)

It is the arrogance of mankind's pride that we see ourselves as able to convert ourselves if we so wished. You can not make your self born-again. The Christian also knows the next truths:

"....for it is by grace you have been saved, and this is not from yourselves, it is the gift of God. " (Holy Bible, Ephesians 2:8)

" This is why I told you that no-one can come to me unless the Father has enabled him ." (Jesus Christ, Holy Bible. John 6:65)

A true Christian then is a person who is born-again, is regenerated . Has had a spiritual resurrection to the heavenly realms.

Let us return to Flatverse: Imagine the Flatties scurrying about their daily business, they have lost all capacity in their minds (souls) for the higher-dimension. They have no awareness of the higher realm. But what would happen if their creator gave to some the three-dimensional life that their souls had lost? If he gave to some spiritual life? The blessed Flatties would become conscious of the higher realm. They would have a different outlook on life.

It would be impossible for them to convince a non-higher- dimensional Flattie, of the reality of what has happened to them (although friends and family would notice a change of behavior and even try to explain the change as an illness).

Remarkably in actual reality the blessed three-dimensional Flatties would be living to some degree in the higher realm.

Their bodies of course would are two-dimensional with their souls inside the body, but their souls also inhabit higher-dimensional space. In other words spiritually, the Flatties would exist to some degree in the higher realm, in the heavenly realms.

Compare these words to born-again believers

> " As for you , you were dead in your transgressions and sin, in which you used to live when you used to follow the ways of this world.......All of us lived among them at one time gratifying our sinful nature (unspiritual nature) and following its desires and thoughts. Like the rest we were objects of wrath. But because of his great love for us , God who is rich in mercy, made us alive in Christ even when we were dead in transgression, it is by grace you have been saved, And God raised us up with Christ and seated us with him in the heavenly realms...."
> (Holy Bible, Ephesians 2:1-6) (parentheses mine)

> " Since you have been raised with Christ, set your hearts on things above....

> .....Set your minds on things above, not on earthly things " (Holy Bible, Colossians 3:1-2)

My friend a Christian can not convince you of the truth of the Gospel of Jesus Christ. I can not convince you that the Bible is God's word. Even if they I had the intellect to put forward reasoned argument based on sound premise and logic, I would not be able to convert you, the greatest writer's at their best can only inform the intellect. You need both an informed intellect, and a supernatural revelation from God. You need to ask God to give you a new heart, for ears to hear and eyes to see.

We can only tell you what we know to be true, Christians know the Bible is the truth. They know this because God in his Grace has given them spiritual life , God through the death of his Son has given the forgiveness of sin. The sin that separated from God has been removed by the death of Jesus Christ. God has raised us with Christ into the higher realm. Armed with this knowledge (both intellectual and experimental) earthly wisdom is not " the measure of all things ".

Christians do not rely on reason alone, but with the very word of God, and the inner guidance of the Spirit, and with the enlightened reason that comes from knowing God, then and only then can we construct a " worldview" that corresponds to reality. We can only write you the truth, we speak of what we know.

> " I tell you the truth, we speak of what we know, and we testify to what we have seen, but still you people do not accept our testimony." (Jesus Christ, Holy Bible, John 3:11)

The knowledge that we have is experiential . We were once dead and knew not God , But now are spiritually alive because we know God. Knowing God is eternal , spiritual life.

> " Now this is eternal life: that they may know you; the only true God, and Jesus Christ whom you sent."(Jesus Christ, holy Bible, John 17:4)

You could reply that it is all in our minds, and you would be right it is all in our souls, for our souls possess spiritual eternal life. You may deny this and say it is not true, and come up with many arguments with which to console and strengthen your unbelief. But the truth is that born-again Christians have spiritual life, they have experiential knowledge of God. Christians can not prove this to you, any more than a three-dimensional Flattie, could prove it to a two-dimensional Flattie.

If in some way you do happen to be convinced of the truth , of the Bible teachings concerning your natural condition, and you do believe that you need to be born-again.

The best that you could manage would be an intellectual assent, for at the end of the day you are spiritually dead.

Only God can help you out of your predicament.

Personal Testimony
(Adapted from the book "The Walls Come Tumbling Down")

The Rainbow People (1982-3)

There is not that single thing in the world, whereof we can know the real nature, or what it is in itself; (Berkeley; 1710; (1981; p216)).

As a young man I worked at a local coal mine, in the Doncaster area.

My life revolved around work and Northern Soul events. After a near death experience involving an accidental overdose of recreational drugs. I began to read as much as I could.

We take up the narrative from my book "The Walls Come Tumbling Down"

My reading material altered. I had moved away from studying science. I concluded that science was trying to explain the *'how'* and even at times it was merely descriptive. I wanted to know the *'why'*. My reading became philosophical. I wanted to know about the nature of reality. I wanted to know about life, death, and the reason (If any) for existence. What was existence?

These were deep questions for a pit electrician to be asking. But the answers I believed where of the utmost importance. Existence, my existence had to be questioned. I had to examine it. I had to examine my being, my life. As Socrates is reported to have said;

...life without this sort of examination is not worth living. (Plato; Apology; 1954; p72)

Was I on a journey of self discovery? A journey to discover what my life was about? Or was I trying to uncover why I always had this awful sense of foreboding, an undercurrent of anxiety.

For some reason I was being driven to find out the answer to these things. I could not rest. I came across the writings of Rene Descartes.

I was extremely impressed by what I read. Descartes a French philosopher published his Meditations in 1641. What struck me about this work was that he wrote as if he was on a personnel journey of discovery. And I could relate to where he 'was coming from'. In his first Meditation he wrote;

> 'I shall then suppose, not the God who is supremely good and the fountain of all truth, but some evil genius not less powerful than deceitful, has employed his whole energies in deceiving me; I shall consider that the heavens, the earth, colours, figures, sound, and all other external things are nought but the illusions and dreams of which this genius has availed himself in order to lay traps for my credulity; I shall consider myself as having no hands, no eyes, no flesh, no blood, nor any senses, yet falsely believing myself to possess all these things; I shall remain obstinately attached to this idea, and if by this means it is not in my power to arrive at the knowledge of any truth, I may at least do what is in my power [i.e. suspend my judgment], and with firm purpose avoid giving credence to any false thing, or being imposed upon by this arch deceiver, how powerful and deceptive he may be.' *(Descartes, 1641: (1990), p303)*

I had never read or contemplated anything like this before. It completely blew me away. 'Wow!' I thought. I quickly read on. In his second Meditation Descartes went on to write,

> 'I suppose, then, that all the things I see are false; I persuade myself that nothing has ever existed of all my fallacious memory represents to me. I consider that I possess no senses; I imagine that body, figure, extension, movement and place are but fictions of my mind. What then can be esteemed as true?' *(ibid ; p303)*

Later in the same Meditation he writes,

> 'Is there not some God, or some other being by whatever name we call it, who puts these reflections into my mind?'*(ibid; p304)*

I was absolutely amazed. Descartes had given me a tool. My *Cartesian tool* would be doubt. I began to read all the philosophy that I could. Where Descartes (and Kant etc) were purely rational, I could use drugs! I would use drugs to discover the answers to these questions. I would doubt what I experienced in the 'real' world. And drugs would be another tool. I would try to *'get behind the phenomena'* of everyday reality. What I perceived as reality (*phenomena*) was caused by something else, something was behind the *phenomena*. Immanuel Kant called this *noumenon.*. Kant claimed that man's speculative reason can only know phenomena and can never penetrate to the noumenon, could never know real nature or the thing-in-itself. (Kant; 1788).

But I was going to use drugs, and not just reason.

One of my work colleagues at Markham main was killed while working down the coal mine; he was dragged into a machine. Peter had only been 31 years old when he was killed. Because of my own near death episode with the 'speed' had shaken me to such an extant that I needed to understand death. I had become fascinated by death. I accepted that one day, any day, I would die. I scoured second hand book shops and stalls for anything related to death and the paranormal.

I was not prepared to just read something, and simply believe it. If what I read could be tested, proved experimentally in someway. Then I would try it out. I would test the things I read by experiment. Rather like the time I had played with the 'Dice-life'. I had read the Diceman book and it seemed like a neat idea. So I tested it by trying it out. I discovered by experiment that dice-living is dangerous. It eventually had a detrimental effect on Will Power and decision making.

I had become acutely aware of my own mortality. To such an extant that I wanted answers, I needed answers. Time and again I would come across occult writings in my studies. Was something else driving me? Pushing me? I also read much about Eastern Philosophy, (Hindu, and Buddhism etc). I realised that there was a 'crossover' between Eastern Philosophy and Occult related States of Mind.

Around this time I had a conversation with a Jehovah's Witness. Something they said struck a cord in me and frightened me. As I tried to analyse the fear that I had experienced while speaking with the Jehovah's Witness, I came up against a brick wall in my mind, what was I frightened of? Was there some memory? Some truth that I could not remember? I didn't understand.

Whenever they knocked on the door I would occasionally invite Jehovah's Witness into my home and have talks with them. But I was not convinced by what they had to say.

Within a short period of time, I had a library of occult and philosophical writings and began to experiment with rituals and Altered States of Consciousness (ASC).

As I read and researched the subject. I discovered that psychedelic drugs could 'create' or shortcut the route to 'spiritual states of awareness' such as those referred to in the eastern philosophical writings. I used eastern meditation techniques, sensory deprivation, drugs, etc. to research my studies into the occult. I would often induce a trance or combine psychedelic drugs with trance techniques.

I had the strong belief that there was something in my mind. That my mind held the key to understanding. Similar to the Greek philosopher Plato's doctrine of 'recollection'. In his early work 'Meno' Plato suggested that all humans are born with innate knowledge; that we are at birth already in possession of knowledge of which we are not conscious.

I firmly believed that my mind held the key, or was the 'doorway' to understanding. What I could not explain was the fear that I kept coming up against. Was the fear a 'false alarm' built in to the human psyche to keep us away from this type of knowledge. Was it a case of only the brave, those that could get passed the fear, would discover the secrets of the human mind? I had to overcome the fear. What was it that the fear was hiding?

One afternoon I was laying on the bed in the spare bedroom. I had closed the curtains but a strong beam of sunlight was revealing the dust in the air. I entered a trance using meditation. I used no drugs for this particular session.

During the trance I had the sensation that I had become 'one' with all that existed. I had became 'one' with the cosmos. I had a very real sense, an awareness, the sensation, that I had filled the universe. I had become 'one' with the universe. My body had become as large as everything. I knew no end. I filled the cosmos.

Later the same afternoon I reflected upon what had happened. I applied doubt to the experience. I had thought that I had become "one" with the universe. I started to break the experience down. During the experience I had not used doubt. But had let the phenomena happen. I looked for another explanation. I began by doubting my interpretation of the whole happening. I eventually came to the conclusion that I had not actually filled the universe, but had actually cut myself off from it. I had *'tranced'* into a condition of sensory deprivation.

Take the sense of touch for example. Touch gives us an awareness of our own extension. We know by touch where we *'end'*; and where the outside begins. But if I had no sense of touch. I would have no *'barrier'* of touch between the outside and myself. In this way the sense or awareness of 'no extension', becomes the illusion of complete extension, the illusion of filling the universe. Because I do not know where I *end* and the outside begins. I become the outside too. If this *'cutting off'* or *closing down* of the senses is multiplied across all our senses, then the illusion is completed. This is what I concluded. I thought that if what I believed was true then Nirvana was such an illusion.

This conclusion was supported by a number of other related experiences. A number of times, I would become 'aware' while being asleep. I would become partly conscious of self, while remaining unconscious in sleep. (This is very difficult to explain, I'm not speaking of sleep paralysis , but a sleep consciousness. I would be in this condition; then quickly regain consciousness through the hypnopompic stage to full awakening.)

I concluded that the eastern philosophical mind state *'Cosmic Consciousness'*, becoming *'one with the universe'* was an ASC, an experience of conscious sleep state; and that Gautama Siddhartha, Buddha had fallen into such a state. That the state of Buddha was not awakening but actually the opposite. Infact an Altered Sense of Consciousness (ASC) that effected the self and the understanding. I therefore concluded that the truth must lay beyond this phenomena.

All the same. I still held the belief that mind; my mind held the key to understanding. And that meditation with other tools could still be useful in my search. As I could use the link between certain drugs, ASC's and occult teachings. I developed a technique of using certain drugs and going into a trance. I was searching for something. I still believed the answer was somewhere within me.

I had read about Astral Projection in a number of occult books and decided to test it out. After about two weeks of frustrating failure I managed to have an experience. I found myself flying down the street. I knew my body was in my bed. After the experience I analyzed what had happened and concluded that astral projection was another illusion, a type of wish fulfilment, a lucid dream. The world in which I was travelling only seemed 'real' while I was in it. When viewed from my normal awake state, the episode was 'dreamlike' having no causal relationships between events;   although during the experience I had believed it to be real.

Sometimes the experiences seemed to give the impression of being more 'real than real'. On the subject of 'Realness' Deikman writes;

> It is assumed by those who have had a mystical experience, whether induced by years of meditation or by a single dose of LSD, that the truthfulness of the experience is attested to by its sense of realness. The criticism of skeptics is often met with a statement, 'You have to experience it yourself and then you will understand.' This means that if one has the actual experience he will be convinced by its intense *feeling of reality*. 'I know it was real because it was more real than my talking to you now.' But 'realness is not evidence. (Tart; (ed) ;1969, p 35).
>
> ~

One Monday afternoon I had a rather potent brew of magic mushrooms. As the 'trip' began. I was determined to control the situation. I would use the method of doubt to keep things in perspective. I said to myself. 'I doubt the existence of the universe'. I started to go into a trance. I said to the whole experience.

'This is an allusion, who, what is behind it? Show yourself'

Immediately a number of beings appeared in front of me. They did not speak. But gave me mental impressions, telepathic communication. They had strangely shaped heads triangular and bird-like. Aliens as we would understand the term. They communicated that they love us, and care for us. And somehow we were their children and they were the gods of this world. I seemed to understand this in some deep and profound way. After a while they vanished and the Magic Mushrooms followed their usual course.

Later as I reflected upon the experience. I was surprised how easily I had believed the whole happening. I was greatly encouraged by the experience. Where these beings real? What about what they had communicated to me. Could we be the offspring of alien entities? Next time I would deny their existence. I would use doubt to gain an even deeper understanding of things.

'I can really get into myself now' I thought.

I kept the whole episode to myself. I knew if I informed anyone about my visit from *'The Rainbow People'* that they would say it was just a 'trip'. But the experience had been 'more real than real'.

This experienced gave me another avenue to research. I read everything I could concerning UFO's and aliens.

~

Sometime later I was watching a TV program, a documentary researching South American Indians. A Shaman was instructing a young apprentice on the methods of entering the spirit world. The Shaman took the apprentice and the camera crew into the forest to a number of sites. He showed the apprentice how to lick certain ants. The ants would excrete some type of acid, and this had a narcotic effect. Later the Shaman made the apprentice drink a special brew, a hallucinatory tea. The apprentice had an experience. Through the aid of a translator he gave details about his experience.

I sat watching the documentary with fascination, the apprentice explained how he had entered into the spirit world and the *'Sky Vultures'* had visited him. The apprentice was asked to describe the *'Sky Vultures'*. He went on to describe in detail the *'Rainbow People'.*

I sat up like a shot. 'Wow!' I gasped.

I thought about what this could mean. Why did the 'Rainbow People' use different names? Could it have been a bad translation by the documentary producers? Could The Rainbow People be the English understanding of their names? I thought the concepts of both vultures and rainbows were far too different to explain the discrepancy between names to be a bad translation.

I concluded that either the experience was a product of hallucinatory drugs, a common drug phenomena and had been interpreted by the users from their own perspectives. T hat somehow certain drugs gave the experience of contact with 'other beings'.

I did not believe in spirits, but did not dismiss the possibility of aliens. The South American Indian lived in a world of 'spirits'. I reasoned the possibility that certain drugs caused the hallucination of these 'beings' and we project onto them our own perceptions. I believed in the possibility of aliens I therefore had an experience of aliens, the Indian believed in spirits so he saw sprits. If my theory was correct, then the 'Rainbow People' did not exist and the experience I had had of them, was also an illusion. But they had seemed so real. What if they were real?

~

I worked on a second theory. Based on the premise that the 'beings' were indeed real. I had what I believed to be a very real experience of other beings. For some reason they had presented themselves in a way that was not contrary to my worldview at the time. But this had to be a deception, a lie. They could not be both aliens and spirits. From my understanding of all that I had read, aliens were physical beings from elsewhere in the physical universe. And spirits were non-physical entities, that were in another realm or another dimension; if they existed at all. I had through my reading of science; I e Carl Sagan come to believe in the possibility of alien life forms, although my scientific research had only presented statistical evidence based upon probability theory.

But spirits? Why would these beings; if they were real, why would they say that they were spirits to the Indian, and say they were aliens to me?

Why had they had lied to me, deceived me into believing that they were aliens? They had appeared to the South American Indian and done the exact same thing. They had reinforced an existing concept of reality. To me they appeared as aliens, to others they appeared as spirits. Why would they propagate differing worldviews?

I thought the second theory, held too many problems. And using the philosophical tool of 'Occam's razor' (The principle of ontological economy; Entities should not be multiplied beyond necessity. In other words; go for the simplest answer). I settled for the former theory. That the whole phenomena was an effect of the drugs onto which we project our worldview, which was an expression of our psyche. But did not completely dismiss the latter.

I had to get to the bottom of this mystery; I had to know the truth.

The Night of the Squatters. (1982-83)

'All the nightmares came today,
and it looks as though they're here to stay; (Bowie; 1970).

One night in November 1982 I had taken a large dose of magic mushrooms.

'Right I can really get into myself this time' I thought. I thought I would try and contact the *'Rainbow People'* and get behind the phenomena, to deny their reality, to discover what it was that projected them into the human psyche.

I felt the 'Mushies' starting to take effect. I closed my eyes. I had to be careful not to be taken up with the effect of the 'Mushies' I had to let it happen, while also observing and directing.

Colours cascaded and kaleidoscoped in my mind. I was part of them. I wanted to stay and play with them, become them. I was the colours. But I had my plan. I had to stay with the plan. I used my will to concentrate on the experience. Not to become too involved with what was happening. I wanted to trace the source of all my experience. The source of my being. The source of the 'Rainbow People' or the source of the illusion. Deeper and deeper.

I began to enter a deeper trance. Answers to questions came as quickly as my questions. Almost as if the answers and the questions were simultaneous. Almost as if I was being directed. The understanding of many things. 'Simple, of course, how profound'

My mind was filling with answers, with knowledge and with power?

Yet deeper I ventured.

A question entered my mind from nowhere, 'what of evil?' 'What is evil?' I opened my mind up to know and understand all that I could..............

'NO' I screamed in silence..

..........In like a flood.

Darkness. Evil. My entire mind filled with evil. Other personalities many of them. I had been tricked. Evil flooded my mind. Other beings, evil beings;

malevolent entities were in my consciousness. Had invaded me. Fear gripped me. I had to escape. I had to surface, to get back to reality. But what was reality? I was in a void a place of chaos. How do I return to reality? I had to get back, I had to get away. I shook myself from my trance.

But 'they' came with me. *'They'* did not stay in the other realm, the realm of magic and mystery. *'They'* came back with me into the reality of the bedroom. I came to myself. I was sweating.

I was petrified, scared. Thoughts filled my mind. I had the distinct sense of being tricked, that I had made a massive mistake. That something beyond terror had happened. My thoughts were not my own. I was being mocked, hated. I could not grasp control of my mind, and the fear increased.

The beings, the evil ones. Many impressions, filled my consciousness. But strangely I knew these beings; they were not strangers to me. They tormented me. Mocked me, hated and despised me. Evil pure evil filled my mind. I tried to block them out. Tried to fill my mind with other things. With other thoughts.

'Think of love, think of love 'I kept repeating to myself. Terrible images filled my mind. Intense fear, panic, terror gripped my heart.

'Think of love, think of love 'I repeated. I ran down stairs. I went to my bookshelf. 'Think of love' I repeated over and over again.

I grabbed one of the books from the shelf, a book that I had had since childhood. A book that had belonged to my mother. For some unknown reason I grabbed the Bible. I opened it at the beginning and read. 'In the beginning God created the heavens and the earth' I read it over and over again. Used the verse as a type of mantra. Using all my powers of concentration to focus upon the words in front of me. Gradually the feelings, the impressions, the awareness of the presence of other beings, faded.

Repeating in my mind, over and over again. 'In the beginning God created the heavens and the earth'. Eventually I fell asleep.

Jesus uses the illustration of a house in order to teach certain points. If I may use a similar illustration. Image that our consciousness is like a house. It has two front rooms, and a cellar.

The cellar represents our subconscious; the front rooms represent our primary consciousness. During the night of Iron and Paper squatters had gained entrance into the house and taken residence in the cellar. When I entered into an Altered State of Consciousness, I would open the cellar door and taken a peak into it. The squatters had tried on a number of occasions to break into the front rooms. But had not succeeded. On this night, I had opened the cellar door and invited the squatters into the front rooms.

The next morning , I reflected upon the previous night's experience 'Boy that was a bad trip' I thought 'but everything was ok now'.

Returning to the house illustration. It appeared that the front rooms had been cleared of the squatters. But something was not right. I laughed off the night's experience as a 'bad trip'. But something had changed. I was not the same. The fear, a fear from long ago, had increased. The squatters where not ransacking the front room as they had done the night before. But they had not gone. They were lurking nearby. They had not completely returned to the cellar. They where hiding in the cupboard, in the one of the front rooms. The cupboard had a hole in it. A hole that led directly to the cellar. In the cellar many more squatters lay in wait.

I had an uneasiness about me, a nagging worry that I could not shake off. The anxiety that I had always has had increased to a creeping fear. I realised that I had a major problem. I had to do more reading I had to research. I had to find out what had happened to me during that 'night of the squatters'. Were the beings real? Or was it a bad trip? I began to read books on psychology and psychiatric writings

I was impressed by the writings of Sigmund Freud. I was especially impressed with his theory of religious beliefs. I read all that the local library had by him. Over a period I read his entire works. I saw some hope for me in his theory of retrogressive fantasy-making linked with traumatic experience. I formulated a couple of theories about what could be happening to me

The first theory was that I had had at some time a trauma. A traumatic experience that I had repressed and as a consequence the anxiety; the fear that was always with me was a symptom of such repression. Freud's *Defence-Neuro-Psychoses* offered an understanding and possibly a way forward.. If I could remember the traumatic experience it would be assimilated and the hysteria associated with the repression would disappear. (Freud; 1893-1908).

My second theory was that I had somehow 'damaged' my subconscious. I had 'given' reality status to something that did not have any real existence. That a 'leak' had occurred in my subconscious and it was seeping into my primary consciousness.

In order to break the power of the illusion. I had to plug the leak. To do this I had to deny the illusion 'to its face'. I thought that if this theory was true, then I would need to conjure again the beings from the 'night of the squatters' and denounce the whole experience as unreal. But I was very extremely frightened of doing this.

When I did try to face the fear, when I did try to deny the illusion to 'its face'; whenever I tried to denounce the reality of the 'squatters' I found that I seemed to only reinforce their existence. It came to the stage whenever I was in a drug induced ASC that I did not have to conjure them into my consciousness the came automatically as if they were with me all the time.

It got to the stage that whenever I took drugs of a hallucinatory nature (i.e. Cannabis, LSD, Magic Mushrooms etc) the 'squatters' would come without my aid. The problem was the more drugs I took, the more times I tried to denounce via confrontation and denial, the more of my mind they seemed to take over.

It came to the point in about Sept 1983 that I stopped using drugs altogether. (Although I did have a couple of joints up to June 1984, but they had the same effect of making matters worse.)

I not only stopped taking drugs, but I also stopped meditating and using occult practices. I just wanted everything to be back to 'normal'. I wanted the fear to go away. If not completely I could live with a little fear. I had had it for so very long anyhow. I wanted the 'sense of the squatters' to go away.

Using our house illustration By Christmas 1983, The Squatters had taken over one of the front rooms. Part of my mind, my consciousness was no longer my own.

I was in a constant fearful condition; I started drinking a lot of alcohol as it lessened the fear. The mornings were the worse. Every morning I would wake up. My first thought would be. 'They are still here' my heart would sink. I hated how I felt. I hated being scared. I hated having to fight 'the Squatters' all day long. I would try and get through the day the best I could. I told no one what I was going through; people would only think I was mentally ill. By March 1984 my condition was becoming desperate.

It was taking a tremendous toll on me; I was trying to keep all this to myself. I dare not share what I was feeling with anyone. I feared I was going insane. I had a constant battle to 'be normal'.

What was my problem? I had to read, somewhere there had to be an answer. These 'beings' can not be real. It must be a mental illness. Yes I had to be unwell.

The Miners Strike (1984)

There is no doubt that the Bible, interpreted in normal fashion, testifies very clearly to the reality and activity of demons. (Dickason; 1987 p 21).

March 1984 Margaret Thatcher put her plan into action. She had been preparing for years to take on the Trade Unions and especially the Miner. I found myself on strike. I tried to throw myself into the strike cause. I went picketing. I tried to fill my life with distraction. I told myself that the problem I had would go away eventually. But all the time it was becoming worse. Being on strike gave me more time to read. I read anything I could that might be of help. Medical books, psychology. Etc.

Nothing I read was of any help. I went into a period of denial. It was as if I had bricked up the room that contained the 'squatters'. I had plastered over the brickwork, and then papered the wall to hide any trace that there was a room even there. It felt as if I had lost half of my consciousness. I even went to the doctors and tried to explain my symptoms without telling him the cause. He prescribed some pills for my anxiety. I never used them.

I was holding the 'squatters' back, by sheer will power alone. I was constantly denying them permission to take anymore of my mind; anymore of my consciousness. What was happening to me? Was I going insane? Was I ill? I was in a desperate, desperate condition.

One day I was sat as usual trying to come up with a solution. Over and over in my mind fighting to remain in control of my consciousness. The idea of suicide had come to me. If things get any worse that is an option I thought. My life was so horrible. The feeling of dread that I had, the terror that was constantly with me was wearing me down. On top off all this I put on an act to everyone that all was ok. I found it difficult to sleep without first having plenty of alcohol.

Discarding The Bible (1984)

It ramifies like a fungus, so to speak, in the dark, and takes on extreme forms of expression, which when translated and revealed to the neurotic are bound not merely to seem alien to him, but to terrify...(Freud; 1990; p 423).

One afternoon in October 1984 I was in the house alone. I was as usual thinking about my problem. It filled my every waking moment. From waking up to falling asleep. Sleep appeared to be the only respite I had. I was desperate; I had tried to deny the situation but this had failed. I still held to my two theories. I tried to remember what the nature of the traumatic experience might have been. I gave up. 'I probably have never had one' I thought.

My second theory, perhaps that is the way out. My second theory was that I had somehow 'damaged' my subconscious. I had 'given' reality status to something that did not have any real existence. But what am I doing wrong'. I puzzled over the problem. Maybe I was giving reality to them by fighting them. Maybe my mind, my will was feeding the illusion. Could it be, that the 'mind time' that I gave to them actually 'fed' or 'gave' them their existence. They were not real; I was giving them 'reality' by thinking about them all the time. 'Yes! That has to be it' I thought with growing hope.

I had for many months now, by sheer will power, kept them from gaining any more of my consciousness. Perhaps if I gave up fighting, this would burst the fantasy. I decided to give it a go. But I was fearful. I had to do it. It would take me hours to *'psyche'* myself up into doing it. I had it all worked out. The delusion was being fed by the *'mind time'*, by the thought time that I gave *'them'*.

All, I had to do was to stop thinking about the problem, to stop using my will to hold 'them' back. And then it would end, like the bursting of a bubble, the exposure of an illusion. It would end, and I would be back to me. I kept repeating my theory to myself, convincing myself that this was the case. After about three hours I was ready. 'Right, I'm ready' I said to myself. 'One,..two,..three' I did it. I gave up the fight. I no longer withheld my mind. I gave up the fight. ....

....In, in like a flood 'they' came. More of *'them'*. Fear, terror, horror and dread filled my heart and my being. I had made another mistake. They flooded my consciousness. Evil, wickedness, many of *'them'*. Again I felt like I had been tricked. 'No' I screamed 'No'.

I did not lose consciousness. But I had allowed more of 'them' to enter. 'They' had gained more of me. I broke down and wept.

I was desperate. I hade made it worse than ever. The terror that was with me intensified. I started to suffer from other strange symptoms. I was in a constant state of 'I'. Strange fantasy filled my mind. Many weird things began to happen in an around me.

For example; I was in town having a walk round, trying to come up with yet another solution to my problem. I noticed an old man mumbling to himself. He seemed mentally unstable. He saw me looking at him. Walked over to me and told me precisely what I had been thinking . It was as if he knew my thoughts. I was losing the plot. I thought that I was going completely insane on the verge of a nervous breakdown, or that I had actually had a breakdown?

A few days later I was sat with my back warming against the coal fire. 'I'm going to make a Doctor's appointment' I decided.. I again went to see my Doctor. I asked to see a psychiatrist. I admitted myself in to the local psychiatric ward. A Doctor interviewed me. I told him my symptoms. He prescribed drugs to help me relax. I refused to take them. I attended two or three counselling sessions, but I thought I knew more about psychology than they did, they were using textbook psychology. I had read all that rubbish and it could not help me. I believed they had no idea what they were talking about, and less idea about what I was going through.

The strange fantasy's that filled my mind were confusing me. Thoughts would come to me and they would seem real. It was as if my imagination had taken on the power to become reality. I was losing it. Losing it big style.

For example I started to believe that the 'Rainbow People' were coming to fetch me. I had to stay awake, go without sleep for a number of nights. Although I was having the strangest experiences. I still held onto my tool of Cartesian Doubt. I knew that what I was experiencing was not real even though at times it seemed 'very real'. I knew that these experiences could not be true. But I was gradually losing touch with what was 'real'. I had these 'beings' in my head, in my mind. They were messing with my mind, somehow manipulating my thoughts and experiences. I was starting to have major delusions.

I kept most of this from the Staff at the hospital. I just wanted a few days rest to sort myself out. This is what I told them. If I had told anyone all that I was experience; I would have been classified as a textbook nutcase.

During the second day I wanted to fill my mind with distraction I picked up the New Testament that was in the cupboard beside the bed. I started to read. I found it difficult. My attention and will power were split between holding back the 'squatters' and trying to understand what I was reading. I was so tired. I had tried to go without sleep for a night or two. I was mentally exhausted, and all the time the terror was with always me. As I read the New Testament I very quickly came across the following words,

> Then His fame went throughout all Syria; and they brought to
> Him all sick people who were afflicted with various diseases and
> torments, and those who were demon-possessed, epileptics, and
> paralytics; and He healed them.'(Matthew 4:24).

This caught my attention. I stopped reading. I re-read it again. 'He healed those who were demon-possessed' I said to myself. As I read and re-read the passage. The print on the paper blurred, the print faded. Obscene images appeared in the print. With horror I threw the Bible away. 'No' I said. 'It's evil'

I sat on my bed, looking at the discarded Bible. 'What happened?'

I questioned myself. Evil suggestions filled my mind, confirming the images that I had seen. I reflected on what had happened? I was tempted to throw my head into the pillow and just weep. The fear filled me, terror gripped me. I was confused. The 'squatters' did not want my thoughts to go to the Bible.

The Walls Came Tumbling Down (1984)

*When evening had come, they brought to Him many who were
demon-possessed. And He cast out the spirits with a word (Holy
Bible; Matthew 8:16.)*

The 'squatters' did not want my thoughts to go to the Bible. I therefore had to
conclude that the spirits were real.

'Evil spirits! I have evil spirits in me' I said to myself with full realisation. At
last I had admitted the truth to myself. Thoughts came rushing in; denying
what I had just come to realise.

'I do, I do know what is true. How could this be true?' I tried to reason it
through. Was starting to believe in spirits now? Had I gone completely
insane? How could I know what was real? I was now believing in demons. I
thought my case was helpless I felt without hope. I had lost all hope of help.

'How do you know what is true?' voices and images filled my mind.

How could I know what was true? At least I had something new to think
about. Something new to go on. I felt alone. I had no help, no hope. I had no
one who could help me. No one would believe me. Everyone would just say I
was mentally ill. I had read all the medical books. I had studied the whole
subject. I had found out the problem, but I was no better off; without an
answer. Still 'they' tormented me; still I held 'them' back.

That night, alone. I reflected on what was happening to me. I ignored all the
strange and evil thoughts. I ignored all the images. I had lost faith in
everything. I could trust nothing. I had lost faith in my life, I had lost faith in
my memory, in reality it self. My faith in life had disappeared. Even now
suicide was not an option. I now believed that evil spirits had entered my
mind. And if this was true I believed that if I died they would get me. What
could I do? To whom, to what could I turn?

After a good number of hours I reached a decision. I would use my 'Cartesian
Tool' I would doubt all things. It was true I did not know what memory, what
thoughts I could trust. I did not know what was real anymore. In fact the
very fabric of reality was falling apart around me. The walls were beginning
to tumble down. I had hardly slept for about a week now.

I had come to the conclusion that if there are evil spirits then there must be good spirits. I knew this was not a logical necessity or even an ethical necessity. But my power to reason was starting to fail me.

For some reason the evil spirits did not want me to read the Bible. So I would read it. I made a decision. I would not believe anything but the Bible. I would doubt all things except the Bible. I would not believe anything I experienced. I would not trust my own thoughts. I would only believe and only trust what I read in the Bible. I began reading the New Testament again. I read what I had read earlier and discovered that it was not an isolated incident. For a few pages later I read;

> When evening had come, they brought to Him many who were demon-possessed. And He cast out the spirits with a word, and healed all who were sick . (Holy Bible; Matthew 8:16.)

I came to passage after passage that said the same or similar thing. That this Jesus had power to cast out demons. I was fascinated I read on into the next portion called Mark. Again the same thing was written,

> At evening, when the sun had set, they brought to Him all who were sick and those who were demon-possessed. (Holy Bible; Mark 1:32).

I read the whole New Testament many times over the next couple of days. Strange thoughts and experiences would occur all the while. But I dismissed them as tricks and illusions to try to prevent me from reading the Bible. Nothing that I heard or saw or experienced I would allow nothing to distract me. I clung to the Bible. 'I will only believe this book' I kept repeating to myself.

Although there was much that I read that I did not understand. I felt I had a good grasp of what the Bible was teaching concerning evils spirits. It taught that they do exist and Jesus Christ has authority over them. As I read and studied the little book I came to see that it taught that Jesus Christ is God and that he was alive.

So I prayed to God, I asked Him. I asked Jesus to deliver me from the evil spirits.

Nothing happened.

'See, it is not true' came the thoughts mockingly with menace.

I ignored everything 'Only the Bible is true 'I repeated.

I cried out 'Jesus, help me please I beg you'

Nothing happened.

I re-read the Bible was I missing something? Some ritual some special prayer, that I had missed? What was I doing wrong? Maybe it was because I have not been as good a person as I ought to have been. 'I can change' I said to myself.

I tried to plea bargain with God. If you deliver me from this God I will do such and such for you. 'I will go to church, I will be good' I prayed. I offered him the rest of my life in service. Nothing. He did not answer my pleas for help. Again I turned to the Bible.

'Help me Jesus to understand this book, help me to do what is required' I prayed. Did I believe he was there? Yes, he must be there the evil ones exist, therefore God must exist. Yes! I knew he was there, I had denied him in word and deed all my life, but now in my hour of need I admitted that I knew that he was there, but why would he not help me?

Crying to him for help, nothing, happened. The demons filling my mind with awful blasphemies against God.

Reading the Bible what had I missed?

Then the penny dropped, I was asking him but not trusting him. Not putting my faith in him.

I asked Jesus to deliver me from this affliction, to heal me. I believed he could and I trusted that he would. Therefore I had to let go, I had to stop fighting against the demons and give it to Jesus.

This was going to be difficult. I had through sheer will power managed to keep them at bay. But now I was tired, mentally exhausted. Tired of fighting. So tired of fighting. I was beaten.

The last time I had stopped fighting. The last time I had let go. They had come in like a deluge. 'Yes but this time Jesus would help wouldn't he?' I said to myself.

I had to trust him. I had to rely on him. Everything else was not good enough. My faith in life had disappeared. I had to have faith in God. To have faith in Christ.

~

I prayed to Jesus I told him what I was going to do. I was going to give up the battle; I was going to hand it over to him.....

.....I let go...

.........He caught me in his arms, like a flash of light, a flood of peace, the Lord himself. He delivered me; in an instant 'they' were gone. 'Gone, gone they've gone.' I cried.

I wept tears of joy. Amazingly, almost unbelievably. My mind again my own once. I could not remember the last time that I had felt normal. 18 months? Two years. Five years longer? Who cares? Now I was me again. I was cured. No demons, no fear, no anxiety.

I had come to the hospital looking for a cure. I had found it in the Lord Jesus. I signed myself out and went home. I was happy. November 1984 I was better. I had been in the hospital seven days and on the seventh day I had found rest.

M freinds thought that I had gone completely insane, talking about God, the Bible and Jesus Christ. I threw away all my books except the Bible. I wanted to understand more about Jesus. I read and re-read the Bible. I thought that I was a Christian. I believed that I was a Christian. I had been delivered from evil spirits by the Lord Jesus but had not trusted in him for salvation

Occasionally I would get attacked by evil spirits, but I would rely on Jesus. Reading the Bible I understood that I was a sinner. I deserved what the evil spirits deserved; I deserved to be cast into hell. I had committed some terrible sins in my life. I had lived a life of selfishness. I had hurt people. I had done many things wrong.

I deserved to be cast into the place prepared for the devil and his angels.

Seated With Him (1985)

But God, who is rich in mercy, because of His great love with which He loved us, even when we were dead in trespasses, made us alive together with Christ (by grace you have been saved), and raised us up together, and made us sit together in the heavenly places in Christ Jesus, that in the ages to come He might show the exceeding riches of His grace in His kindness toward us in Christ Jesus. (Holy Bible; Ephesians 2:4-7).

In March 1985 I went on a protest march to London; the Greater London Council was being abolished by the Prime Minister Margaret Thatcher. The year-long miners strike was over. But my Colliery was still on strike. It would only be a week or so before we returned to work. I attended the protest I was paid £5 pounds by the Miners Union for attending. I had too much to drink that day, I got shamefully drunk.

The next day at home. I prayed to Jesus. I asked for forgiveness for my drunkenness, for my sin. I asked him to be my Saviour. And not to let me go ever. I asked him to save me. I asked him to forgive me.

I got up from praying. I was not sure whether I was forgiven, I still felt guilty.

'Don't trust how you feel; believe what the Bible says' I thought.

I went down stairs. I sat down....

I had my back to the radiator warming myself. I was reflecting on what the Bible says about being forgiven in and by Jesus.

Suddenly the Spirit of God came upon me. Joy, Peace filled my heart, filled my entire being. Jesus came to dwell in the house. He filled the two front rooms. He filled the cellar, he filled my very being.

I knew at that moment that I was forgiven. I knew then that I would never be lost. I knew then that I was seated in the heavenly realms with him. I had a most wonderful experience of assurance. And afterwards I was filled with joy, filled with the peace that passes all understanding. I knew Jesus Christ, knew him empirically.

I had an almost overwhelming experience of the presence of Jesus Christ. He was with me, and I was with him. Too this very day he has not left me.

I had been cured, and now I was forgiven. But how did I know this? Had I replaced one delusion for another. Was I still unwell as my friends believed?

I thought about the whole experience. I reflected upon it. How did I know it was of God? How did I know it was from Jesus? How did I know that my sins were forgiven. How did I know I was seated in the heavenly realms? How did I know that the whole experience of Christ was not another illusion? Again using the 'Cartesian Tool. I carefully reflected on these questions, I reflected on my wonderful experience.

'I know these things are true because Jesus tells me in the Bible that they are so,' I said to myself.

'And the Spirit of God bears witness with my spirit that these things are true'

My experience was of Jesus Christ, was confirmed in the Bible.

I had come into a personnel relationship with the risen Christ.

You may read this testimony and know something about me, about my life and experiences. But at the very best all you will have is knowledge about me. For you to know me in an empirical manner; you would have to meet me in person. More than that; you would have to have a personal relationship with me. This is what had happened I had come into a personal relationship with Jesus, he is alive and I know him.

I knew then that I had to bring every thought captive to Christ. Jesus had delivered me from the powers of darkness; he had delivered me from occult bondage and subjection. More than that, he had delivered me from the very kingdom of Satan and translated me into his very own. He had forgiven me my sins. I love my God because he heard my voice. Yet in despair I thought my end was near, my faith in life disappeared.

The Hymn by JM Barnes which is based on Psalm 116 is one of my favourites.

I love my Lord because He heard my voice.
My God, He listens to my prayer.
Because He hears me
When I call on Him.

Through all my days I shall pray.

My soul was saved from death; my eyes from tears.
My feet now walk before the lord;
Yet in despair,
I thought my end was near.
My faith in life disappeared.

What can I do, to thank God for His love-?
For all his benefits to me?
I will lift up salvation's cup on high
And call on Him by name.

My vows to Him I promise to fulfil,
To Him I sacrifice my life.
He freed me from the servitude of sin
And now I serve as His slave.

Unite in praise, great family of God
His children bring to him your thanks.
City of peace, where God has made his home
With one accord, praise his name.

Adler Mortimer J (ed); 1990; Essay on the Mind; in the Syntopicon, an index to the great ideas; Great Books Of The Western World, Vol 2, Chicago: Encyclopaedia Britannica.

Berkely George; 1710 (1981); The Principles of Human Knowledge; Collins / Fontana; Glasgow.

Davis Paul; 1989; The Cosmic Blueprint; Unwin Paperbacks ; London.

Descartes, Rene;1641: (1990), Meditations on First Philosophy, translated by Elizabeth S Haldane and G R T Ross, in Mortimer J Adler, ed., Great Books Of The Western World, Vol 28, Chicago: Encyclopaedia Britannica.

Dodds E R: 1951; The Greeks And The Irrational: University Of California Press: Los Angelas.

Edwards Jonathan; 1834; (1986); The Works Of Jonathan Edwards; Two Volume Edition; Banner of Truth Trust; Great Britain

Frank Anne - The Diary of Anne Frank (The Definitive Edition) Kindle Edition

Freedman Daniel X & & Dyrud, Jarl E. [eds]; 1975American Handbook of Psychiatry Vol 5; Basic Books.

Gleick James; 1987; Chaos; Cardinal; London.

Hale E; 1983; New York Times magazine, April 17.

Hawking Stephen; 1995; A Brief History Of Time; Bantam Books; London.

Hume David; 1748; (1990) ; An Enquiry Concerning Human Understanding; edited by L A Selby-Bigge; in Philip W Goetz (ed);

Great Books Of The Western World, Vol 33, Chicago: Encyclopaedia Britannica.

James William; 1990; The Principles of Psychology; in Philip W Goetz (ed); Great Books Of The Western World, Vol 53, Chicago: Encyclopaedia Britannica.

Kant Immanuel; 1788; (1956); Critique of Practical Reason; translated by Lewis White Beck; The Bob-Merril Company, Inc; New York.

Kierkegaard Søren; 1843; (1987); Either/Or ; translated by H V Hong & E H Hong; Princeton University Press; New Jersey.

Lindsay A D; 1919; The Philosophy of Immanuel Kant; T Nelson & Sons Ltd; London.

Luntley Michael; Wittgenstein: Opening Investigations May 2015

Nietzsche Friedrich; 1891; (1997) Thus Spake Zarathustra; Wordsworth Editions Ltd. Great Britian.

Nystul M S; 1987; " TM " in Concise Encyclopaedia of Psychology, edited by R.I Corsoni . New York: John Wiley and Sons.

Plato; Apology; 1954; (In The Last Days of Socrates; 1988) ; Penguin Classics; Penguin Books, Great Britian.

Sagan Carl;1980; Cosmos; Macdonald; London.

Sire James W; 1997(third edition); The Universe Next door ; IVP ; Leicester, England.

Skinner B F; 1967; Science And Human Behavior; The Free Press; New York.

Trueblood D Elton; 1987; The Philosophy Of Religion; Baker Book House; Michigan.

Warnock G.J, (ed): 1967; The Philosophy Of Perception; (Oxford Readings In Philosophy Series); Oxford University Press; London.

Wittgenstein Tractatus Logico-Philosophicus (Routledge Classics) 2001

Wolf Robert Paul (ed); 1967; Kant, a collection of Critical Essays; University of Notre Dame Press; Notre Dame.

31241657R00066

Printed in Poland
by Amazon Fulfillment
Poland Sp. z o.o., Wrocław